SOUTHEND
AT WAR

SOUTHEND
AT WAR

DEE GORDON

The
History
Press

This book is dedicated to Donna Lowe and Debbi Campagna as a thank you for all their support, enthusiasm and assistance over the last years, especially as 2009 was not a great year for either of them

First published 2010
Reprinted 2013

The History Press
The Mill, Brimscombe Port
Stroud, Gloucestershire, GL5 2QG
www.thehistorypress.co.uk

British Library Cataloguing in Publication Data.
A catalogue record for this book is available from the British Library.

ISBN 978 0 7524 5262 3

Typesetting and origination by The History Press
Printed and bound in Great Britain by
Marston Book Services Limited, Didcot

CONTENTS

INTRODUCTION AND ACKNOWLEDGEMENTS

Southend at War is the result of a lot of conversations with Southenders and a lot of visits to local museums, libraries, memorial sites and the Essex Record Office, as well as time spent on websites and emailing questions to all kinds of experts – collectors, curators, military organisations, historians and writers.

Arthur Foster, Mave Sipple, Kim Kimber and Chris Bailey (among others) provided leads, and the search for photographs was assisted by www.clipart.com, Ken Crowe (Southend Museums), Ian Boyle and www.simplonpc.co.uk, Peter Brown and www.thesoutheastecho.co.uk, Ronald Wordley, Kelvin Baldwin, Mik Glen, April Pearson and Michael Harrington. Norman Gillett was exceptionally prompt with information about Roy Ullyett and with providing images. Similarly, writer Frances Clamp was particularly co-operative in providing contacts and allowing the use of material, as was Councillor Steve Aylen. Information sourced from the internet (e.g. the excellent www.southendtimeline.com) was verified with either the appropriate organisation (e.g. the RAF or the Commonwealth War Graves Commission), or with databases such as Answers Direct, with local archives and newspapers, or with 'specialists' (e.g. Southend's Macebearer, Keith Holderness).

Apart from those entertaining Southenders who have been happy to have their own stories included, my thanks obviously go to all the others mentioned in the text. In the end, I had – sadly – more anecdotes and stories than I could use.

The press cuttings and archives (*Southend and Westcliff Graphic*, *Southend-on-Sea and County Pictorial*, *Southend Standard*, *Essex Countryside*) at Southend Library had a lot of information with regard to the area during both world wars, and the staff were always ready to lend a hand accessing and verifying this material.

Dee Gordon, 2010

PART ONE: THE FIRST WORLD WAR

CHAPTER ONE

THE TOWN

At midnight on 4 August 1914, there were crowds outside the offices of the *Southend Standard* waiting for news of England's declaration of war on Germany following the unprovoked invasion of Belgium. One of the odder impacts of this declaration locally was the directive that Southend and Leigh-on-Sea pubs should close by 9 p.m. (some sources suggest as early as 6 p.m.). However, the evening trains to nearby Eastwood (to the west) or Rochford (to the north) carried more evening travellers than usual because the pubs there could remain open till 10 p.m.

Lord Kitchener's famous recruitment campaign (Your Country Needs You) culminated in a grand rally at the Kursaal, and over 1,000 men were sent to France and over 400 others joined the territorial forces. By November, twenty-two Southenders had already been killed.

When the townspeople heard what sounded like a bomb on 26 November, the worst was feared. In fact, the 15,000 ton Royal Navy battleship HMS *Bulwark* moored on the other side of the estuary (at Sheerness) had exploded when her magazine was ignited accidentally while being loaded. In total, over 700 officers and crew lost their lives in the explosion, with a handful of survivors seriously injured.

The confidence of Southenders was displayed – with tongue perhaps in cheek – in the *Southend and Westcliff Graphic* of 1 January 1915, with an illustration of the town's Mayor announcing:

> We in Southend haven't much to fear with such patriotic men as the special constables willing to pace the night through, and with our national guard drilling for all its worth and ready to face with martial ardour a landing should it be attempted. Southend can rest in its bed.

Quite.

The main power plant and sub-stations in the town were boosted by the council's acquisition of half a dozen diesel engines from – ironically – German submarines that had come into governmental hands.

A First World War Zeppelin. (www.clipart.com)

According to the *Southend Standard*, Southend-on-Sea was on the receiving end of the first air raid in the country – although Dover makes the same claim, for Christmas Eve 1914. The report is probably a reference to a German taube (an early mono-plane), which caused some excitement when it was seen above the Thames on Christmas morning, 1914. On 28 December 1914, *The Times* reported an air attack on Southend, with one 'intrepid' airman fought off by three biplanes in a 'wonderful aerial combat'. However, the first Zeppelin raids took place on 19 January – and not too far away (at Great Yarmouth).

Local councillor, Steve Aylen, claims that 'the first enemy aircraft shot down over Britain' crashed into the Thames on 1 April, 1915, after halting over The Elms at Leigh-on-Sea – although not quite long enough for the Royal Flying Corps to attack it – but this story has not proved verifiable. He also describes other reports of Zeppelins passing over the town on 13 April 1915.

Southend was hit by well over 100 bombs in one of the first real air raids in this country on 10 May 1915, but the pier – an obvious target – escaped, although it, and the prison ship moored alongside, had close shaves. The first explosion occurred in York Road, partly damaging a house in which a soldier was billeted. The second landed in Ambleside Drive, missing houses but shattering windows and blowing open the door of Councillor Iles's house. The third bomb landed in the roadway at Cobweb Corner – and the rest were incendiaries.

London Road bomb damage. (Author's collection)

Although the town managed to avoid serious damage, houses in London Road, West Street and Baxter Avenue that experienced direct hits from incendiaries were virtually destroyed. Such incendiaries, and their resultant fires, did damage in Ceylon Road and Richmond Road, while others dropped on the cliffs and the beach. At one point, fifteen fires were lighting up the town, six of them on a large scale, keeping the local fire brigade very busy. Local fire-fighters were hampered by the lack of water pressure available during the night, and by the unexpected size of the demand on the service.

There was one fatality (a senior Salvation Army member, Mrs Agnes Whitwell, asleep in North Road), and a full account was published in the *Southend Standard* and elsewhere, including *The Times* and the *Daily Mirror* whose headline read 'Huns Havoc at Southend!' Attached to one of the bombs found in Rayleigh Avenue, Southend, was a scrawled message, also featured in the press:

You English we have come and will come again soon – kill or cure.

The 1,200 interned German civilians on the SS *Royal Edward* had a lucky escape and must have been unusually grateful for the inaccuracy of the German Zeppelins. Less lucky was Flaxman's timber yard in Southchurch Road, which was badly damaged by fire.

Above: Flaxman's timber yard. (Courtesy of Duncan Cooper)

Left: West Street damage. (Ronald Wordley collection)

The Zeppelin LZ.38 was the first Army ship to attack England, commanded by Hauptmann Erich Linnarz, but he only got as far as Canvey Island when anti-aircraft fire turned him back.

Later that month (26/27 May), a further seventy bombs hit the town – again thanks to Hauptmann Linnarz, who was exploring the easiest route to London. This time there were a further two female fatalities, a young girl (in Broadway Market) and a visitor (Miss Fairs) who was tragically hit by falling shrapnel from an anti-aircraft gun when in Southbourne Grove. Naval fire at Shoeburyness was instrumental in stopping the Zeppelin from unloading even more devices.

Major Linnarz and others involved in the Zeppelin raids were regarded in their own country as heroes, of course, as pictures in an early *Daily Express* reveal. Perhaps not too surprisingly, however, there was a lot of anti-German feeling in Southend. Shops sporting German-sounding names – Tragdrof, Ernst, Wertheim, Zucker, Hermann – were attacked by rioters.

By September 1915, the Southend branch of the Anti-German Union in Weston Road was up and running with 700 members. A similar message was being conveyed in some newspaper advertising: 'British Toys for British Boys' declared Trafalgar Toy Manufacturing in Nelson Street over Christmas, advertising scale models of British warships made by 'our warriors broke in the wars'. Even the Sisters of Notre Dame, a German order at St Mary's

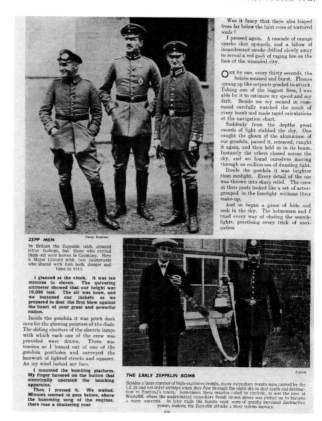

Was it fancy that there also leaped from far below the faint cries of tortured souls?

I pressed again. A cascade of orange sparks shot upwards, and a billow of incandescent smoke drifted slowly away to reveal a red gash of raging fire on the face of the wounded city.

ONE by one, every thirty seconds, the bombs moaned and burst. Flames sprang up like serpents goaded to attack. Taking one of the biggest fires, I was able by it to estimate my speed and my drift. Beside me my second in command carefully watched the result of every bomb and made rapid calculations at the navigation chart.

Suddenly from the depths great swords of light stabbed the sky. One caught the gleam of the aluminium of our gondola, passed it, retraced, caught it again, and then held us in its beam. Instantly the others chased across the sky, and we found ourselves moving through an endless sea of dazzling light.

Inside the gondola it was brighter than sunlight. Every detail of the car was thrown into sharp relief. The crew at their posts looked like a set of actors grouped in the limelight without their make-up.

And so began a game of hide and seek in the sky. The helmsman and I tried every way of eluding the searchlights, practising every trick of navigation.

ZEPP MEN
In Britain the Zeppelin raids aroused bitter feelings, but those who carried them out were heroes in Germany. Here is Major Linnarz with two lieutenants who shared with him both danger and fame in 1915.

I glanced at the clock. It was ten minutes to eleven. The quivering altimeter showed that our height was 10,000 feet. The air was keen, and we buttoned our jackets as we prepared to deal the first blow against the heart of your great and powerful nation.

Inside the gondola it was pitch dark save for the glowing pointers of the dials. The sliding shutters of the electric lamps with which each one of the crew was provided were drawn. There was tension as I leaned out of one of the gondola portholes and surveyed the lacework of lighted streets and squares. An icy wind lashed my face.

I mounted the bombing platform. My finger hovered on the button that electrically operated the bombing apparatus.

Then I pressed it. We waited. Minutes seemed to pass before, above the humming song of the engines, there rose a shattering roar.

THE EARLY ZEPPELIN BOMB
Besides a large number of high-explosive bombs, many incendiary bombs were carried by the LZ.38 and her sister airships when they flew through the night sky to deal death and destruction to England's towns. Sometimes these missiles failed to explode, as was the case at Westcliff, where the undetonated incendiary bomb shown above was picked up to become a mere souvenir. In later raids the bombs used were of greatly increased destructive power, making the Zeppelin attacks a most serious menace.

First World War National Press coverage. (Ronald Wordley collection)

Convent in Milton Road, Westcliff, returned to Germany, being replaced with French nuns by 1918.

A later Zeppelin (2 April 1916) passed low over the pier and crashed into the Thames, brought down by anti-aircraft batteries at Purfleet. This was also the year when Southend Water Company's reservoirs at Belfairs Park were targeted, leaving plenty of craters, but the reservoirs undamaged. Other incidents included one at Shoeburyness, on 5/6 June 1917, when two were killed, and twenty-nine wounded.

The Gotha bomber attack on Sunday, 12 August 1917, was the worst to hit the area, with around forty bombs dropped in fifteen minutes from twenty aeroplanes. This time, as no air-raid warning had been given (the Gothas had seemed to be on their way to London), there were a lot more fatalities (more than thirty), the majority near to what is now Southend Victoria railway station, with over forty injured. The fire brigade on this occasion was not only busy with hoses putting out fires, but also with washing away the signs of slaughter, and moving bodies before the general public were exposed to the unpleasant sight.

A piece of one of these bombs, dropped on what was then the technical school at Victoria Circus, and inflicting extensive damage, is in the possession of David Knight from Thorpe Bay. Similarly, he holds a piece of a raiding Gotha brought down at Rochford in December 1917.

From hereon, Southend avoided any further multiple bombings, partly because of the improvement in local anti-aircraft defences, and also because the focus of attack shifted to London – although the worst air raid of the war (19 May 1918) did mean a handful of bombs dropped on Thorpe Bay and Shoeburyness, luckily causing little damage.

PRISONERS

The *Ivernia* (mainly occupied by German military), the *Saxonia* and the *Royal Edward* (both for civilians) were moored off Southend with nearly 5,000 prisoners. The prisoners, mainly 'aliens' including titled Germans, did not necessarily stay for the duration of the war, being moved on to other forms of internment. The ships remained until 1915 when they were moved to more obvious war work.

One of the larger houses then in Victoria Avenue (later to become Westcliff High School for a number of years) was used as a POW 'camp' for German officers. They could be seen exercising in the grounds from the upper floor of the trams that passed along the avenue.

Different kinds of prisoner were absentee conscripts, such as William Henry Kirby of Moseley Street, one of whose brothers had been killed in France. He was found hiding under a bed in May 1916 by a policeman, then fined £2 and handed over to the military.

German prisoners of war arriving in Southend, 1917. (Author's collection)

SOUTHEND'S HOSPITALS

Early in the war, Queen Mary gave her patronage to establishing a naval hospital in the town. Messrs Tolhurst, the owners of the Palace Hotel, offered the building rent-free for the duration of the war. This was particularly generous given the hotel's status as the only five-star hotel on the south-east coast, built with its own winter garden and palm court. The landmark building has recently undergone a glamorous renaissance.

HM Queen Mary's Royal Naval Hospital had its first intake in October 1914, when 168 Belgian soldiers arrived by train, with wounded soldiers from the British Expeditionary Force following soon after, including victims of Ypres.

By March 1917, over 4,000 British soldiers and sailors had been treated, although only sailors were admitted after that date. The number of beds increased from 220 to 350 to cater for the unexpected numbers of wounded arriving after the Battle of Jutland. Incidentally, the white ensign of HMS *Marlborough*, torpedoed in this particular conflict (with a number of Southend sailors aboard), can be found inside St John the Baptist Church in the town.

Patients were kept busy making bags, nets, jerseys for wounded comrades, shawls and all manner of handicrafts. Hospital balconies overlooked the pier and the estuary so that patients could not only benefit from the fresh air and the views but could also lower tins on string to the people below who would fill them with cigarettes, sweets and money!

This hospital was mainly staffed by nurses from the Voluntary Aid Detachment (VADs) apart from three doctors and the matron. It seems to have had one of the first made-to-measure X-ray departments in the country, if not in the world – although at

HM Queen Mary's Hospital. (Author's collection)

Wounded sailors at a Southend hospital. (Courtesy of Southend Museums)

this stage there was no protection for staff. The eleven wards had such topical names as Kitchener and Russia, and some of the press pictures at the time show the stark contrast between the utilitarian hospital beds and the elaborate chandeliers in rooms which were once used as ballrooms and lounges. The property reverted to its former use in 1919.

The Glen in Southchurch Road, previously a holiday home, was converted by the local branch of the Red Cross (the first Red Cross hospital in the borough), as was the Overcliff Hotel on the Leas. By 1917, most of the Army patients had been transferred to the Overcliff. Other public buildings were similarly utilised (e.g. Porter's Grange), and there was a supply depot for 'war hospitals' in Hamlet Court Road.

A few miles away, the 'aged and infirm block' at Rochford Hospital was used for accommodation for German civilian POWs and their guards from May 1916.

The town's cottage hospital in Warrior Square was especially busy following the August 1917 Gotha raid. Supplies of iodine were quickly exhausted and local chemists were called upon to top up supplies. Some of the doctors, trying to get to the hospital, used the only transport available: a milk float.

An organisation known as the British Sportsmen's Ambulance Fund stepped in to present the town with three ambulances, which were well received.

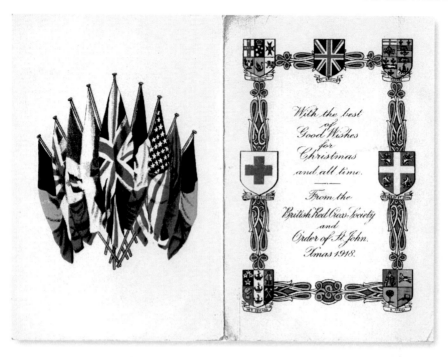

A Red Cross Christmas card of the First World War. (April Pearson collection)

This year I've guns and carriages,
And military marriages;
Plum puddings, lots of baccy,
For warriors clad in Khaki;
Some push for the boys that are brave,
And some ships for the ocean wave.
I've lots of Camaraderie,
And the certain hope of VICTORY!

I'm sad for the boys that are gone,
But I say, none the less, "CARRY ON!"
Carry on against odds that are mighty
For the sake of dear old BLIGHTY.
Brave hearts, I cry, Better Cheer,
Please God, I'll bring PEACE NEXT YEAR.

Interior of the Red Cross Christmas card. (April Pearson collection)

Queen Mary. (Author's collection)

Royal Visits

Several royals visited the town during the First World War, the first visits since Princess Charlotte 100 years earlier. Queen Mary visited in June 1914 at the opening of the hospital named after her, and HRH Princess Mary visited in July 1917. When the princess arrived she was greeted by thousands of children from the local elementary schools lining up along the cliffs, with some of the pupils assembled at the bandstand to present her with gifts – including a bag of onions. The crowds, the flags and general air of celebration were perhaps a little at odds with what was going on in France.

Because so many of the early casualties at Queen Mary's Hospital were Belgians, Princess Clementine of the Belgians also visited the town, in 1915. As well as expressing her appreciation of the work of the Red Cross, she visited Chalkwell Park and was entertained there by the band of the Royal Garrison Artillery.

Defence

The first anti-aircraft guns on the cliff-top – and at nearby Shoeburyness Garrison – did not have a good enough range to do any real damage to the Zeppelins. More active deterrents were the fighters of the Royal Flying Corps and the Royal Naval Air Service, with specially formed Home Defence squadrons.

On the ground, air-raid shelters were provided for the public by utilising larger schools and venues such as the Palace Theatre. Trenches were dug in such locations as Belfairs Farm, occupied by members of the 4th Battalion Essex Regiment – Southend's National Guard unit, a fore-runner of the Home Guard.

Troops stationed in the area were given permission to use the parks for drills and parades. The 14th Rifle Brigade had to comply with one condition before they could use Southchurch Park: keep away from the cricket pitch!

THE EMERGENCY SERVICES

The fire brigade had a special role to play during the war years – between 1914 and 1918 they had to stand by during the progress of raids on 130 occasions. Sometimes this meant the crew members had to be in readiness at locations in Southend, Westcliff and Leigh for four or five hours at a time, and sometimes they had to be on call for the whole night. Several members of the brigade assisted abroad in Red Cross work or joined the forces, and many auxiliary firemen were appointed for 'work of national importance'.

H.E. Johnson, a First World War fire-fighter. (Ron Nicols collection)

At the outbreak of the war, the Southend-on-Sea County Borough Constabulary (formed in 1914) had just two horses and three bicycles at their disposal, along with a green Humber for the Special Constabulary.

Local jeweller and generous philanthropist, R.A. Jones, introduced the Perpetual Ambulance Challenge trophy in October 1915. This was to be an annual competition between squads representing the St John's Ambulance Association and the British Red Cross Society in Southend-on-Sea.

TRANSPORT

Seven new-fangled single-decker buses had been purchased by Southend Corporation only months before the outbreak of war. As a result, the War Department made use of three of these. The diminished service was finally laid to rest in 1916, partly because of the unreliability of the remaining four vehicles and partly due to the financial losses that had been incurred. This meant that no buses were seen sporting Southend's livery for a number of years, although the town's trams did continue to operate.

The railways were prioritised to carry equipment and troops for four years, finally reverting to normal excursion traffic.

CHAPTER TWO

THE PEOPLE

SOUTHEND'S CHILDREN

When Daisy Kebby's father was serving in Constantinople, her mother took on a bigger house, sharing it with another fatherless family. She was having her seventh child at the time, and Daisy was just five when they moved into a rented house in Park Lane, Southend – quite a rural part of central Southend, backing on to what is now Southchurch Park (previously Wiffins Farm). Although so young, Daisy remembers the pinky-red décor, lit by gas mantles, with a bit of a shudder. She has fonder memories of the blacksmith's next door and a 'bushy tree' in the garden.

Southend Education Committee made an order compelling schoolchildren to remain in their classrooms during air raids, the last of which was on Whit Sunday 1918.

Pupils at Southend Technical School got involved by growing vegetables and also made crutches, bed screens and thousands of splints for the Red Cross. Schoolgirls at Chalkwell School knitted mittens which they sent to France even though, because their knitting styles were different, the mittens were odd sizes. Gunner Neill of the 15th Brigade Expeditionary Force sent a thank you letter in March 1915 assuring them that they were 'just the thing to keep our hands warm these cold mornings'.

Pupils from North Street School sent eggs for the patients at Queen Mary's Hospital, an egg being considered a meal. Gladys Wayland, aged seven, was awarded the Empire Day Certificate for this service.

Air-raid precautions notice. (Peter Brown collection)

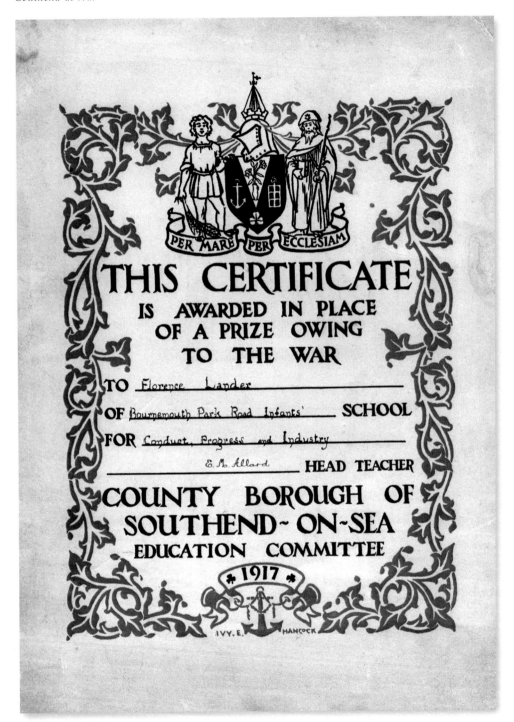

Southend Education Certificate. (Courtesy of Southend Museums)

Young Jim Ballard, aged ten in 1915, had rather different 'jobs' during the war. He lived in a suite of the Palace Hotel because his father was the hotel's accountant who also looked after the finances of the Royal Naval Hospital Trust. Jim would help the sailors by buying coloured silks in the High Street for their embroidery, or wheel them uphill to the Strand cinema.

THE ARMY ON THE DOORSTEP

The 65th Searchlight Regiment were based at the drill hall in East Street, Prittlewell, with the stationmaster's house used as regimental headquarters. The searchlights, incidentally, threw the light of 1,000,000 candle-power intensity, but, because the sound locators were pretty crude, it wasn't always easy to separate friend from foe – until radar came along.

Other soldiers, billeted locally, took to target practice in Heygate Avenue, where dummy bullets were fired at painted targets on the wall of The Cloisters, a detached house which had started life as the 'parsonage' for St John's Church. They also taught local boys to use a Short Lee Enfield rifle bolt and to roll up puttees (the strips of cloth used as leggings).

For 2nd Lieutenant Groombridge of the Leicesters, death came as a tragic accident in November 1915. When passing the brigade HQ in York Street on his motorbike, he felt obliged to return the guard's salute, colliding with a cyclist in the attempt. The accident resulted in a fractured skull, and a funeral with military honours.

Following a meeting of the trustees in September 1918, the Wesley Hall in Elm Road, Leigh-on-Sea, was designated as a Soldiers' Institute for a battalion about to be stationed

Above: Searchlights over Southend. (www. clipart.com)

Right: The stationmaster's house. (Courtesy of Peter Brown)

in the area. It seems that, because a large number of soldiers were Wesleyans, 300 'Active Service hymn books' were purchased for their use, at eight shillings per hundred.

SOUTHENDERS AT WAR

When war broke out, 'Jimmy' Nichols saw the news in a newspaper while at the hairdressers in Canada (where he had emigrated from Southend-on-Sea to become involved in the burgeoning motor industry). He hurriedly returned (to West Road) and signed up for the Army, who were setting up a Motor Corps – having previously used horses. As there were very few soldiers who knew as much about motor maintenance as Jimmy, he was promptly shipped to Greece to work on the vehicles of the Ambulance Corps.

The very first British battleship to be torpedoed and sunk by a German submarine (1 January 1915) was HMS *Formidable*, with at least two Southend men aboard. Seaman G.E. Saker of Westborough Road was one of the lucky ones to be rescued, but nineteen-year-old Private Charles Jones of Whitegate Road (a member of the Royal Marine Light Infantry Unit) lost his life along with over 500 others. Twenty-nine-year-old Able Seaman Philip Moore, from nearby Great Wakering, was also one of those drowned.

HMS *Formidable*. (Author's collection)

On 14 May 1915, Private Cecil Cattell from Leigh was, at sixteen, the youngest soldier in the Essex Yeomanry to die in the First World War. He had enlisted on the first day, 4 August 1914, leaving behind his family in Leighton Avenue when aged just fifteen. His end came in the second battle of Ypres in an attack on Frezenburg Ridge, and he is commemorated on the Menin Gate memorial as well as locally.

In September the same year, the *Southend and Westcliff Graphic* proudly announced that Mr and Mrs Hull of London Road had received a letter from the King, congratulating them on having five sons in the Army: three sergeants, a lance corporal, and a driver. Whether the Hulls felt as happy about the situation is not recorded.

A rather overly optimistic North Benfleet man, Revd P.J. Loseby, a rector and a corporal with the RAMC in France in 1916, sent home a letter claiming that 'when you read our casualties you will bear in mind that about 80 per cent of the wounds are very slight, and will be healed in about a month or even less'.

Later that year, a report in the *Southend and Westcliff Graphic* announced that Lieutenant L.S. Lee, a member of the Westcliff Yacht Club, had obtained a first-class certificate at the Imperial School of Bombing Instruction in Cairo, and was now a brigade bombing instructor in Egypt. Well done that man.

Leonard Smart of Southend-on-Sea was one of many who saw active service in France. He joined the Durban Light Infantry Pioneer Battalion because, as a builder, he knew that the pioneers were responsible for a lot of the building work required in France, e.g. supporting trenches, building temporary bridges, etc. Before the war, he had planned on being an architect's draughtsman, but he received a shrapnel wound in his right shoulder and was invalided out, returning to building work and following in his own father's footsteps.

Twenty-year-old Frederick Gale, who had been working at Schofield and Martin (the grocer's) in Alexandra Road and living in lodgings at St Olive's, York Road, joined up two weeks after war was declared. As a member of the 9th Battalion of the Essex Regiment, one of the first to answer the call for volunteers, he became part of 'Kitchener's Army'. He was sworn in on 6 September 1914 with three other Southenders. Their first parade was

First World War RAF poster. (Author's collection)

First World War Army poster. (Author's collection)

outside the town's recruiting office, with an enormous crowd of people who had gathered to see them off, and with the band of the Irish guards to lead them to the station. There the Mayor of Southend made a speech and the chaplain from Shoeburyness Garrison gave the boys an emotional blessing. A special train was waiting at the platform, with a lot of girls on the platform ready to be kissed. According to Frederick's diary, 'I think I kissed about twenty or thirty girls in the few minutes we were waiting' – and the new recruits played cards and sang all the way to Brentwood station, *en route* to Warley Barracks. Their favourite song was 'A Long Way to Tipperary'.

His diaries cover the 1914 training period at Dovercourt and Aldershot, and when he eventually got his uniform and equipment (which took several months) Frederick went across from Folkestone to Boulogne to the front line. Here the diaries stop, although he did scribble a brief note of crucial dates and events on the back of a Player's cigarette packet. This reads:

August 30 1914 – June 1915 Training in England
June 1915 – Jan 1917 – France
June 1915 Plugstreet [colloquialism – this was for trench training]
Sept 25th 1915 Loos
Oct 13th 1915 Hohenzollern Redoubt – wounded
Dec 15th from hospital, back to unit
April 1916 Monchy le Preux
July 3rd Somme [where 9th Essex lost 400 of 900 men]
Nov 20th 1917 Cambrai [45,000 British killed here by 7 December]
Dec 1st Captured
Dec 1918 Back to England

The injury he received – a shell in his buttocks – was only part of his medical problems. Not unusually, there was also trench foot, frostbitten ears and mustard-gas poisoning to contend with. Being captured was a great improvement on the alternative – being shot – and Frederick felt that he avoided the latter by taking the opportunity to remove a Red Cross armband from a dead comrade and putting it onto his own arm, suggesting that he was a stretcher-bearer, and therefore perhaps more eligible for a reprieve.

The camp at Westphalia in Germany had far superior provision to that offered by many others, so Frederick continued to count himself lucky. There were regular football matches and there was a billiard room and even an English library. Clothing, however, was scarce and inmates (of all nationalities) wore whatever they could beg, borrow or steal. Food was in short supply, and survival was dependent on Red Cross parcels (despite a general aversion to pilchards!) … and a sense of humour. Frederick survived the war and returned to his old job, weighing less than six stone. Like many, he spoke little in later life of his experiences.

The *Southend Standard* took upon itself the grim task of reporting the names, week on week, of the thousands of servicemen missing and dead throughout the war years – many reports were accompanied by photographs.

Right: Frederick Gale (central figure with
V-neck jacket) at Westphalia Camp. (Dennis
Gale collection)

Below: Westphalia Camp billiards room.
(Dennis Gale collection)

CIVILIANS AT WORK

Women came to the fore during wartime, displaying hidden talents. Vital work included cultivating previously redundant land and pea-picking, as well as replacing men in offices, banks, the railway, the Post Office and on the trams. Additionally, fifty women applied for employment when the local electricity works in London Road, near the town centre, was converted into a munitions factory.

Female messengers replaced telegraph boys at the Post Office in 1917, and were supplied with a smart blue uniform decorated with red piping and brass buttons, topped with a dark straw hat with black and red ribbons. The fifteen girls employed were expert cyclists.

Nurses were obviously in great demand, but few sacrificed their lives in the way Ellen Daly did when she set her clothes alight while cooking for patients at Southend Sanatorium in March 1915. Although she put out the flames unaided, and carried on with her duties despite being severely burned, she collapsed and died from her injuries and shock just a few hours later.

OUT FOR VICTORY.

THE ALLOTMENT HOLDER.
Too old to fight, but doing his bit to beat the U boats.

OUT FOR VICTORY.

THE MUNITION GIRL.
"England expects every woman to do her duty."

The importance of allotments in the First World War ... and the importance of munitions and the female work force. (April Pearson collection)

Fundraising ladies in Southend, First World War style. (Author's collection)

Less dramatically, members of the Borough of Southend Needlework Guild were busy making sandbags for the soldiers at the front and holding open-air working parties to promote their cause. Women farm labourers at the Salvation Army colony in Hadleigh took the place of male labour, loading up hay carts and stacking hay on the elevators, although hampered by their flowing skirts.

Volunteers were employed at Prittlewell Sewage Works when it converted to making shells, while 250 men volunteered for the special police and over 100 joined the Southend branch of the National Guard, who attracted admiring spectators when drilling in local parks. The largest voluntary organisation locally was the Volunteer Watch, which formed in 1915 following the first Zeppelin raid. The Watch had 2,500 members in the area, meaning that virtually every street had its own patrol.

Even local Scouts were able to help in soup kitchens, with patrol duties, assisting coastguards and, especially, running messages. They could also blow whistles, hooters and their bugles as air-raid warnings.

Professional men were involved in different kinds of war work. Local dentist E.H. Richards, of 124 High Street, advertised himself in wartime newspapers by suggesting that 'Your teeth demand attention during the present national crisis'.

Then there was a Mr Tumnidge who, in peacetime, was a sail-maker in Leigh-on-Sea, but switched his skills to a government contract for khaki tents for troops, even though this required the installation of special machinery.

The wood, parks and nature reserve provided plenty of timber for wartime coffins. Local coffin makers dug sawpits in Belfairs woods (Leigh), traces of which can still be found.

The uniform of the 3rd Westcliff Scouts during the First World War. (Courtesy of Michael Harrington)

CIVILIANS AT PLAY

Life during the First World War was not all gloom and doom. In 1915, the Warrior Square Picture Theatre offered such light relief as *How Lieutenant Daring Saved London* and the newly-built Palace Theatre at Plough Corner featured comedies such as *D'Arcy of the Guards*. The town also boasted such venues as The Hippodrome and the Empire Theatre, with additional entertainment at Shorefield Gardens, and open-air concerts in Happy Valley on the cliffs at Westcliff-on-Sea.

The town's new municipal open-air swimming baths, measuring some 300ft by 70ft, opened in May 1915. The pool held 560,000 gallons of water, and was immediately popular.

Southend's premier department store, Keddies, came up with a patriotic display for its window – a warship made out of hundreds of folded handkerchiefs.

War brought a wider interest in horticulture, resulting in a record entry (of 340) in the Horticultural Society's show in August 1916 at Shoeburyness. Similarly, 1,700 forms were issued to allotment holders in 1917, with 100 acres of the borough thus utilised. It seems that there was a large demand at that time for potato seed, and crops were grown on parts of the golf courses at Rochford and Thorpe Hall.

Open-air swimming pool, Westcliff sea-front. (Author's collection)

During 1915's August bank holiday, the town had a record influx of 100,000 visitors, enjoying the new pool and existing attractions such as the Kursaal Gardens, with free admission for soldiers and sailors. Although the main Kursaal buildings were used as billets for the troops, the eleven acres of amusements remained open. A new feature installed at this juncture was a facsimile of a section of the trenches at Ypres, and an exhibition of incendiary bombs which had been dropped on the area by Zeppelins. The Rifle Range, it seems, came in useful for local regimental practice. A year later, a zoo was added with such exotica as eagles, a panther and ostriches. One of the most bizarre war relics exhibited (August 1916) was advertised as 'Step inside to see the brains of a German'. The admission fee (3d) allowed you to see the remains of said brains clinging to the inside of a German officer's helmet which had been pierced by a bullet, killing its wearer.

War did not seem to have an adverse effect on visitors – although carrying a camera could have you arrested as a spy. One couple who married in Ilford in 1916 came to Southend for their honeymoon, and liked it so much that they moved a year later to Retreat Road, Westcliff, only moving back to Ilford when the war was over. This couple, incidentally, were Mr and Mrs Thompson, with the latter (and her lover) being hanged in 1923 for Mr Thompson's murder!

February 1918.   1st London. (Royal Fusiliers)   b'uck

Above: Stanley Giddins, one from left. (April Pearson collection)

Left: An article written by Stanley Giddins, 'The Most Expensive Soldier'; printed in the *Evening Standard*. (April Pearson collection)

The Most Expensive Soldier

I do not, of course, claim to be Britain's youngest disabled soldier of the Great War, though I am probably one of the youngest, having joined the Army at 17 and been discharged at 18.

I do claim, however, to have been the most expensive soldier in the ranks.

For my *effective* war service (i.e. for the period I was actually in the Front Line) the cost at the approximate rate of £1,000,000 per annum.

I base my claim on the following calculation. I entered the Front Line and went over the top around midnight on August 23-24, 1918, and again at 4.30 p.m. on August 25th. On the latter occasion I was first wounded in the left arm and later my left leg was smashed to bits by a 9.2 shell. Thus *effective* service equals one and three-quarter days!

For this one and three-quarter days my cost to the country has been or will be approximately £4700! i.e.

		£	s	d
(1)	Training and upkeep in England, including attestation transport, instruction etc say	30	0	0
(2)	Equipment, clothes, arms, etc say	20	0	0
(3)	Transport etc to the front line, including food and ammunition	10	0	0
(4)	After wounds: Hospitals (C C S Peronne, Rouen American Hospital, Cosham (Hants), Hayling Island, Woolwich, Roehampton), including transport, food, nursing, attendance, three surgical operations (not to mention my "special" food of cream and port wine, etc at Hayling Island V A D say	250	0	0
(5)	Artificial limbs (approximately a dozen at, say £20 average)	240	0	0
(6)	Other attendances for repairs and/or treatment (including "in-patient" periods) during the last eighteen years	75	0	0
(7)	Eighteen years travelling and subsistence and "lost time" allowance, Roehampton and elsewhere, say	50	0	0
(8)	Army pay and gratuity	50	0	0
(9)	Estimate of annual cost on a "pro-rata" basis for recurring items (5,6 and 7) for the next 30 years, say	500	0	0
(10)	Disablement pension (for 50 to 60 years). I have already drawn it for 18 years and I am now only 37 and in good health, say	3500	0	0
	Total	£4735		

Thus £4700 for one and tree-quarter days' service is equal to an annual rate of roughly £1,000,000!

S.C.C.Giddins
(late 1st London R.F.)
Great Eastern Avenue, Southend-on-Sea

CHAPTER THREE

THE PIER, THE GARRISON, THE AIRPORT

Before the outbreak of war, the 3rd Battle Squadron of the Home Fleet anchored off the pier before moving to their battle station at Portsmouth. A war signal station was set up at the pier-head, paid for by the Admiralty.

Tugs were used to transfer prisoners from the pier-head to the Cunard liners moored further out to sea which were used as prison ships. Thus, the pier became more of a war zone than the rest of the town, but escaped severe damage.

Post-war, the enemy submarine *Deutschland* was placed on exhibition at the pier-head to raise money for King George's Fund for Sailors.

Although on the outskirts of Southend-on-Sea, at Shoeburyness, the garrison's activities impinged on the resort, not least because it was responsible for firing nearly two million rounds of ammunition. The Border Regiment at Shoeburyness was needed to protect against invasion and sabotage and other units were drafted in, including the Rifle Brigade which was billeted in the Kursaal. In August 1914, the School of Gunnery and the Royal Horse and Royal Field Artillery Schools were closed, because experienced officers were needed overseas – but as this made the officer shortage worse, the Schools were re-formed in 1915.

As a school for anti-aircraft instruction, the garrison was important enough for King George V to visit in 1916, when schoolchildren were given a day off. It was also used as a transit camp for soldiers on their way to the trenches in France, and the attached theatre was turned into a hospital during the war years.

Because of the on-site ammunition stores, and the nature of the testing, there were occasional disasters. At least half a dozen lives were lost during the war years due to accidents with guns – not enemy action. Another disaster was the ammunition fire in 1918, which set off explosions that could not be controlled for some twenty-four hours and led to a large-scale evacuation of the Southend area and a serious loss (as much as £3 million worth) of supplies.

Britain was seemingly the last country to set up an official dog training school, thanks to the persistence of well-known dog trainer, Lieutenant Colonel E.H. Richardson.

He and his wife moved to Shoeburyness pre-1916 and sought out suitable dogs, many from dog homes which were overflowing due to the food shortages. Offers of dogs eventually came in from 7,000 owners, to the apparent amazement of the War Office. Training involved the necessity to frighten the animals with the sound of explosions, but within a week their hunger overcame their fear and they were happy to come out of their kennels during 'bombing' rather than miss out on meals. They were introduced to all the hazards they were likely to encounter – burning haystacks and barbed wire, crowds, busy streets, shell fire and machine guns. Many such dogs, acting as messengers, battled on after being gassed or wounded.

Known locally as Southend Airport, the airport at Rochford (north of the town) saw some service during the First World War when several squadrons defended against attacks on London and East Anglia. The site was acquired for the military in 1914, as a landing ground for the Royal Flying Corps, and became the largest flying ground in Essex. It was ideal both in its location at the mouth of the Thames – the main gateway to London – and in its geological make up as a flat well-drained meadow, previously given over to buttercups and potatoes.

Initially used for training, the airport soon became a front-line station once Zeppelins started bombarding Southend (and elsewhere) in 1915. The airport was taken over by the Royal Naval Air Service who set up camp at the corner of the site, near to the church and trees.

Many defence sorties were made during 1915 and 1916 when Zeppelins appeared overhead *en route* to London, with Home Defence squadrons formed specifically to counter the Zeppelin threat. The RNAS moved out in June 1916 and RFC Rochford took over what was now classified as a flight station for night work. Interestingly, it seems that the on-site accommodation for ground staff was still not finished by November 1916, meaning that billets in Rochford had to be utilised, with aircrews based at the Westcliff Hotel on the seafront. Duty crews had to be driven from the hotel to the aerodrome when an alert came – as it often did (for example, on 28 November).

In 1917, deadly Gotha bomber raids produced more than a dozen sorties by the end of the summer, although at least one was as late as December (5th). Within a year, Rochford was operating as a night training station and an anti-aircraft experimental sub-station.

Although the airport could only claim one successful 'capture' (a Gotha which crash-landed on the nearby golf course), it became the largest in Essex, acquiring a reputation as 'the most comfortable billet in the RAF' according to such noteworthy air aces as Cecil Lewis, the author of *Sagittarius Rising*, who was stationed there in transit. At that time, it was described as modern, magnificent, and on a grand scale. A shame then that, after the military left, it reverted to farmland, with crops hiding its runways.

Not long before the end of the First World War, two squadrons were formed at Rochford: a home defence unit in January 1918 (141 Squadron) and a Camel fighter unit in October (152 Squadron), who moved to France soon after to defend allied bases against enemy night bombers. The difficulties for these early airmen included open cockpits, resulting in ice forming on their clothes at 22,000ft as the oxygen diminished.

CHAPTER FOUR

A TEMPORARY PEACE

The siren at Southend gasworks signalled the end of hostilities in November 1918. Celebrations erupted all over the town, with the most notable being the Victory Ball at the Kursaal. Local airmen paraded in heavy rain, thanksgiving ceremonies were held in the town's churches, and the seafront was ablaze with colour. Although police were in evidence, they turned a bit of a blind eye at the revelry.

It wasn't until 19 July 1919 that Peace Day was celebrated on a grand scale. In the Thames, the battleships from the Atlantic and Home Fleets laying off Southend for a celebratory week fired a twenty-one-gun salute followed by a fireworks display. The crews from these battleships, cruisers, submarines and destroyer were special guests at events all over the town, and the Lord Mayor of London put in an appearance. Some of

Illuminated Fleet, Southend on Sea. July 19TH. 19

The illuminated fleet off Southend, 1919. (Author collection)

the ships welcomed aboard visitors; an unforgettable experience for a number of lucky members of the public.

Other celebrations included a carnival procession with traditional donkey rides and Punch and Judy for the children. Priory Park hosted a garden fête and at night the fleet moored in the Thames was illuminated in spectacular fashion. Peace medals were issued by Southend Borough to local schoolchildren at a special ceremony.

Southend United Football Club moved to new grounds behind the Kursaal in 1919. Their original base, Roots Hall (formerly Roward's Hall Fields), had been ploughed up for potatoes. Another local club, Great Wakering Rovers FC, was established the same year by demobbed soldiers who were working in the local brickfields.

Postscript: The manager of the Southend Hippodrome (in Southchurch Road), one Walter de Frece, became a Sir in 1919 following his wartime service. A Conservative MP, he was married to the world-famous music hall artiste Vesta Tilley.

PART TWO:
THE SECOND WORLD WAR

The illuminations went out in Southend on Sunday, 3 September 1939, after just two weeks' display, after Neville Chamberlain's chilling announcement that Hitler could 'only be stopped by force' following his invasion of Poland. A declaration of war was bound to have a dramatic effect on this vulnerable town at the mouth of the Thames Estuary. The Thames was the route to the London Docks, the largest port in the world, and a pointing finger to the country's capital clearly visible from the air.

As the announcement came, the funeral procession of Southend's Mayor, Herbert Dowsett, was leaving Porters, the official mayoral residence. The Bouquet Concert Party at the end of the pier had to break off their performance, and the next day dangerous animals in the town's zoo at the Kursaal were 'humanely dispatched' (as per the *Southend Standard*) in case their cages were damaged and they escaped.

A parade of troops, guns and tractors that had been planned by Southend Council for 17 September was cancelled because of the timing, although the resort was actually better prepared than most because it had been tested earlier that year for the effects of blackout. The local drapers had made a lot of money providing black cloth to seal up the town's windows, and senior members of the military and the civil service came to watch how the inhabitants coped. From as early as June 1939 the local papers were carrying instructions about air-raid shelter construction and appealing for people to join the ARP services. Even before that, gas masks were being issued to adults and children – gas masks which were never used, and whose cardboard boxes fell to bits within weeks.

Southend-on-Sea had to adhere with wartime East Coast Regulations, becoming first a restricted area and then a defence area. Residents were told to pack a suitcase ready for the invasion, because in that event they would only have one hour's warning to get to the station. By 1940, the town had been allocated 17,000 Anderson shelters and 140,000 gas masks had been issued – the latter an extra duty for the police, with schools mainly used as allocation centres.

EVACUATION

Although children from London were evacuated to Southend in 1939, it was not regarded as a 'safe house' for very long. Notices were displayed from the 21 June 1940 on every public noticeboard and pillar box and in shop windows all over Southend:

You Should Take Precautions Now To Ensure That You Could Leave At Short Notice.

Evacuation, Southend style. (Courtesy of Southend Museums)

This prompted over 84,000 residents to leave within the next few weeks, the population dropping sharply from 135,000 to around 15,500 – although they started to return in less than six months. Anyone in the furniture removal business would have done well. Although there was an element of choice where evacuation was concerned, it was not an option for pregnant women who 'had' to go, partly due to the shortage of doctors in the town.

CHAPTER ONE

THE TOWN

The town looked very different after several years at war. Only a few families and key-workers were visible on the streets, which were mainly occupied by men and women in uniform. The streets were empty enough to encourage the return of wild rabbits to the town and railings were removed from around the town's parks and from such locations as Hamlet Court Road bridge.

Troops were billeted in private homes around the town, which accommodated in total around 600 officers, 5,000 men and 700 WRENS. Dining halls were built on tennis courts behind the Grosvenor Hotel in Grosvenor Road, and there were two mess huts on Chalkwell seafront and two huts set up for ENSA concerts. Schools were used as ARP posts, and there were gun emplacements in picturesque locations such as Belfairs and Thorpe Bay. Outlines of some of the gun emplacements can still be seen, incidentally, around what is now Belfairs golf course, and are particularly evident from the air.

By 1941, the Thorpe Hall golf course was being used as a firing range for grenades (presumably the cows allowed to graze there had been moved on!) and part of the Belfairs course at Leigh was also requisitioned by the military. Anti-aircraft guns were mounted in every Southend park and open space as well as along the pier and on specially built forts in the estuary.

The beach was cordoned off with barbed wire, and Michael Harrington of Eastwood (Leigh-on-Sea) remembers his mother telling him that she was fined 10s for bypassing the barbed wire to take him, in his pram, onto the beach in 1943. There were also nearly 2,000 unsightly tank traps (concrete blocks as big as 6ft wide and 7ft tall) along the sea wall from Chalkwell station to Thorpe Bay, plus cook-houses and ablution blocks along the promenade – not the stuff of picture postcards.

Leigh Harbour remained accessible because of the fishing fleet, the boat building (of Johnson and Jago) and the Thames barge traffic, so local children made good use of this 'facility'. They had been deprived of their paddling pool alongside the pier, which was eventually covered with green algae.

Wartime fire appliance. (www.thesoutheastecho.co.uk)

The fire service became nationally important and was re-branded as the National Fire Service. In Southend, they took over a row of shops near The Bell public house (Prittlewell) and became the headquarters of the No. 11 Fire Area, with an extended force (male and female) during the war years. The service also had temporary locations around the town, including Kent Elms corner, Tylers Avenue, Elm Road (Leigh), and St Augustine's Avenue. During the Blitz, Southend fire-fighters would travel further afield to deal with oil fires on Canvey Island or dock fires at Tilbury.

For blazes more centrally located, a brick-built reservoir was erected in Warrior Square to provide extra water supplies during air raids, and there were other reservoirs in Hamstel Road and in Milton Road, Westcliff.

The beaches – especially around Shoeburyness – were deliberately mined and sailing was banned. Photography was forbidden on the seafront and local newspaper photographs had identifying landmarks obliterated, or replaced by images produced by war artists. The use of field glasses was banned and pleasure boats were given a coat of camouflage paint.

An ack-ack gun on the pier. (www.thesoutheastecho.co.uk)

The arches at the foot of Shorefield Gardens, which started life as summer chalets and are now popular bistros and cafés, had a different role to play during the Second World War – they were used as ammunition dumps for troops billeted in the terraced houses nearby.

Residents would have found it hard to escape the military influence even if they wanted to. Some cinemas, such as the Mascot in London Road, showed primarily instructional films, and even the open-air swimming pool on the seafront was utilised in teaching sailors how to swim – or at least stay afloat – this skill not being an essential requirement when signing up for the Navy. Football and cricket pitches at Belfairs were used for troops to exercise, and Belfairs Park had a sentry guarding one of its entrances to keep 'fifth columnists' out. Mobile ack-ack guns became a common sight around the town.

This time, the Kursaal, and its 'Kinema', closed – from June 1940. The fire brigade used the water chute as a reserve water supply, and even the ballroom appears to have been used for military purposes – as a NAAFI store – probably responsible for subsequent cracks in the floor.

In case it was needed, a carriage was reserved for German prisoners on a daily train from Shoeburyness to Fenchurch Street. A Nissen hut camp was erected for them at Wakering Common, with Italians nearby at Oxenham Farm, Wakering. These prisoners were given quite a bit of freedom, being allowed to work on local farms, and seemed to cause no problems. Similarly, German POWs were moved into wooden huts constructed in Danescroft Drive, Leigh, which offered very limited security.

Should members of the public in Southend want a close look at the workings of an AA gun, one was installed in the grounds of the Municipal College at Victoria Circus. Others looking out past the pier during 1942 would have seen dummy ships made of plywood to divert enemy air attacks. Mik Glen's mother remembers the barrage balloons suspended from barges and ships, which, during a storm, could be seen descending in flames following a lightning strike.

The trolleybus extension from the Kursaal to Thorpe Bay (initiated in June 1939) was unfortunately timed, resulting in immediate cutbacks in the service. A single set of wires had been erected around Warrior Square for the trolleybuses, and route numbers were finally introduced in March 1944, although the numbers did not actually appear on the vehicles for another five years! Trams ran as far as Leigh-on-Sea early in the war, but their tram-lines were taken up to help the war effort and were replaced by trolleybuses on the

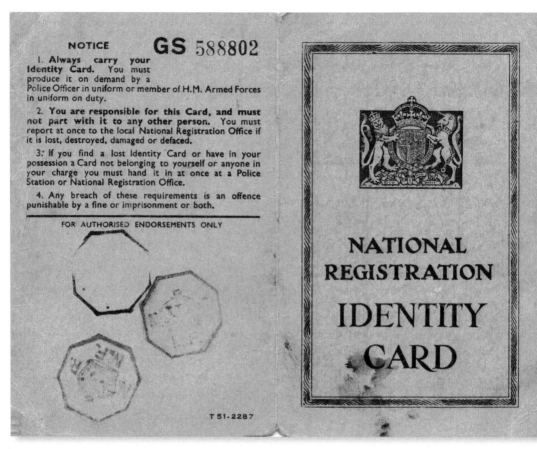

A wartime ID card. (Peter Brown collection)

same routes. The last local tram ran, in celebratory fashion, from Porter's (the Mayor's official residence) to the depot on 8 April 1942. More unusually, a gas-driven omnibus owned by Westcliff Motor Services was introduced between Pier Hill and The Plough (by October 1940).

Trains from Southend Central and Southend Victoria stations did continue to run, following the requisite blackout regulations, although they were occupied more by troops than civilians. Local coaching services carried warnings reminding travellers to Southend, Rochford, Rayleigh, Eastwood and Benfleet that these areas were in a restricted coastal zone. 'Passengers travelling to these areas must be residents or hold an official permit' and 'no refund' would be payable if a passenger was ejected by the police, who were at liberty to carry out spot checks on all vehicles travelling east of Dagenham. Anyone without a local address or without official business was turned back. Even members of the Salvation Army Band were stopped to have their ID checked.

The absence of the necessary paperwork was taken very seriously. In January 1941, one Eileen Kirby, described as a twenty-two-year-old 'wayfarer', was found in an air-raid shelter in Southend without such permission. As a result she was sent to prison for three months 'for entering a defence area without a permit'.

Another issue was the difficulty of making a telephone call. A waiting time of up to three hours was not unusual because available lines out of Southend were given to police calls as priority. The police presence in the town had been boosted, of course, by the Police War Reserve, attracting around 100 extra pairs of hands.

Rationing, as elsewhere, made demands on the housekeeping skills of the women left behind. Many shops, such as Woolworth's in the High Street, remained open throughout the war years, as did Garon's, a well-known name in the town.

All Southend signs had to be removed to 'fool' the enemy and vehicles and shop hoardings had to have the word 'Southend' obliterated. When the paint faded, however, revealing the name underneath, no action seems to have been taken, so

SOUTHEND-ON-SEA, ESSEX
Rationing of Foodstuffs

1. The address of the Southend Food Control Office is 118 Victoria Avenue, situate on the same side of the Avenue and about 100 yards north of the L.N.E. Railway Station. Phone Nos 68181, 68182 and 6380.
   Those who intend to go away for a holiday, and to do their own shopping while away, should apply to the Food Office in their own home district for Emergency Ration Cards.
3. Application should be made to such Food Office during the week previous to their holiday, and applicants should take with them to the Office their Ration Book with any pages of coupons which may have been deposited with retailers. If the coupons for the period of their holiday are intact, these coupons will be cancelled at the Food Office before the Emergency Card is issued. If, however, any coupons for the first week have already been used, corresponding coupons will be cancelled on the Emergency Card before issue. If the holiday extends into several weeks, Emergency Cards will be given, covering not more than six weeks, if desired, subject to the cancellation of the coupons in the Ration Book for those weeks.
4. Although Emergency Cards may be obtained at the Food Office of the place where the holiday will be spent, visitors will find it quicker and more convenient to apply to their local Food Office.
5. Those who have booked rooms at an Hotel, Inn, or any other accommodation which is licensed by the Ministry of Food as a Catering Establishment will not need Ration Books with them on their holiday. If holiday-makers do not know whether their accommodation has been so licensed they should apply for Emergency Cards as a matter of precaution. They may, however, save themselves trouble if they ask for details of any classification when booking rooms.
6. Visitors remaining in the Town for five or more consecutive nights and staying in an Hotel or Boarding Establishment, holding a Ministry of Food Catering Licence should hand their Ration Books to the Manager or Manageress Visitors staying in Private Apartments not licensed as a Catering Establishment should hand their Emergency Cards to the Proprietor. If, however, they do not intend to have their meals at the place at which they are staying, they can obtain meals at Restaurants, etc., without surrender of Ration Coupons.
7. Visitors staying for less than five days, unless staying at an Hotel, or Boarding Establishment holding a Ministry of Food Catering Licence, should bring their own rationed commodities with them, or take their meals in Restaurants as indicated in paragraph 6.
8. In all cases, if pages of coupons have been deposited with retailers, they should be recovered and fixed securely in the Ration Books before coming away.
9. Owing to the present supply position, visitors would be well advised to bring their own towels.

N.B. The above is subject to any subsequent alteration of the Rules and Regulations of the Ministry of Food.

Issued by the Corporation Publicity Department, Southend-on-Sea.

7/46

Rationing notice. (Author's collection)

this may well have been over-reacting. Restrictions were imposed on the movement of cars and motorcycles, and over a million sandbags appeared (courtesy of the Borough Engineers) to protect public buildings – council offices, the police station, the waterworks, first-aid posts, fire stations, and air-raid shelters.

Obviously, self-sufficiency came into its own during the war years in Southend. Everyone left behind seemed to keep chickens, and some also had rabbits, or even bees for honey at teatime. Gardens had space to grow potatoes or provide fruit from established orchards and the public parks were called upon to provide vegetable plots. Southchurch Park had glass-houses to boost the output from its 20,000 tomato plants, Chalkwell Park replaced flowers with turnips and broccoli, Shoebury Park produced onions, carrots and beetroot, and Priory Park had space for 200 'Corporation' chickens which produced between 5–600 eggs every week. Even the cliff-tops at Westcliff were not wasted – photographs of the area in the *Southend-on-Sea and County Pictorial* show flourishing crops of spring greens. The *Southend Standard* provided some fascinating information on how many vegetables were grown in the first year of the war alone:

6,500 pounds of tomatoes
2,500 cucumbers
6,000 lettuces
3,500 bunches of radishes
3.5 tons of potatoes,
1,000 cabbages and cauliflowers
4,800 pounds of beans and peas
48,000 carrots
12,000 beetroot

Rossi's ice-cream, now widely famous, had established itself in Southend-on-Sea by 1939, but the main outlet at 1 Marine Parade had to close when the military intervened. Pietro Rossi, the Italian patriarch of the family and the business's founder, was interned to a camp on the Isle of Wight as an 'alien'.

Some idea of the significant shortage of fruit and vegetables can be gauged from the front page of the *Southend-on-Sea and County Pictorial* on 9 August 1941. Was it about air raids? No, it announced that: 'Yes, we have some oranges', with the cover story confirming that 350,000 oranges had arrived in the town depot in Campbell Road, Westcliff.

Everyone was encouraged to save 'for after the war', with a boom in National Savings stamps. As for books, they became a valuable resource, and a local 'book drive' was initiated in 1943 resulting in 36,250 volumes being sent out to the forces and a further 16,500 being requisitioned to replace those lost by bombed libraries.

THE HOSPITALS

Some of the land surrounding Southend's main (general) hospital, in Prittlewell Chase, was given over to orchards and crop growing. The building, together with the smaller Rochford Hospital (for maternity and obstetrics), were partially emptied, with patients (and nurses) moving inland, leaving accommodation for war casualties. Converted Southend Corporation buses were used to assist in taking patients to safer areas. The restaurant in Belfairs Park became a temporary mini-hospital for a while and extra blood donors and stretcher bearers were recruited.

The blackout was a problem area for Southend's hospital and its many windows, although staff worked together to prevent even the merest crack of light escaping. In all, some 86,000 sandbags were used to protect the building. However, by 1940 when it became one of several coast defence hospitals, with civilian accommodation reduced to just 100 beds, the sandbags were replaced with blast-proof walls around wards.

Bombs landed close by, but missed the main building. One hit a gas main and one a water main and telephone cables, which, although causing obvious problems, could have been so much worse. Plans had been made to use Fairfax School in the event of enemy damage, but this does not seem to have been necessary. In July 1940, the nurses at Southend Hospital organised a dance for pilots and ground crews from Southend Airport, and this had a special guest, namely Godfrey Winn, the journalist and broadcaster.

In 1941, a Military Camp Reception Station took over much of the ground floor but, by 1943, 200 civilian beds were available, although maternity and gynaecological patients were catered for elsewhere. There was an ante-natal clinic in Warrior Square, for example.

Interestingly, many of the staff reluctantly took an intensive course of German because it was quite common for wounded members of the Luftwaffe to be treated in Southend.

Apart from the hospitals, a few temporary first-aid posts were erected around the town. The largest of these opened in December 1942 in Guildford Road. This had its own ward and operating theatre underground for extra protection, with twenty-five staff in evidence.

THE CHURCHES

On the Sunday morning when war was declared many were at church. At St Mary's in Prittlewell, the vicar, Canon Gowing, passed the bad news on to his congregation shortly after 10 a.m. St Mary's was one of several churches that lost most of its choir-boys following the mass evacuation of schoolchildren from Southend.

Although many churches gave up on evening services during the war, St Mary's did not because the vicar had arranged for enormous blackout blinds to be made. This particularly enterprising vicar also arranged for the stunning stained-glass seventeenth-century Durer window to be removed and hidden in the cellar of the nearby vicarage in West Street. In July, 1943, this was the church that hosted a BBC broadcast to the men of Southend

Princess Mary, in her ATS uniform, and Canon Gowing at the opening of Women's Services Club, Wilson Street early in the Second World War. (Courtesy of Linda Barnard)

Wesley Methodist Church plaque. (Author)

serving in the Middle East – a broadcast which included the church bells chiming, rung by a proud Mr Frank Lufkin.

Further east, one Welsh regiment billeted around the Southchurch Park boasted a Welsh padre, and he sometimes took the local Sunday service at Southchurch Park Congregational Church.

Many local churches set up canteens for the local troops, and laid on entertainment. St John's Church hall (close to Pier Hill) was requisitioned for use as the Naval Control Service's social club, known as The Ship's Club, with entertainers such as Frankie Howerd. Canteens included the old iron Methodist Church (at Belfairs, Leigh), Clarence Road Baptist Church, and York Road Methodist Church, with additional facilities such as billiards and a writing room at Avenue Baptist Church.

The Wesley Methodist Church in Elm Road, Leigh-on-Sea, also removed its stained-glass windows at the outbreak of war. The window spaces were darkened with removable shutters because of the shortage of blackout material, and its old hall was blacked out by the Scouts and Boys' Brigade. The premises were thrown open as a community centre, with seventy women volunteers helping to run the social club catering for the troops. By 1944, it had served up well over two and a half million meals.

HELPING OUT THE TROOPS AND THE ALLIES

The foyer of the Southend Astoria in the High Street (later The Odeon) displayed photographs of Southenders serving in the war (1941) headed 'War Effort'. This was an attempt by National Savings to appeal to cinema-goers to stick a 6*d* saving stamp under the

Above: Sweet Melody and some of the crew.
(Peter Brown collection)

Right: War Weapons Week featured in
Southend-on-Sea and County Pictorial.
(Author's collection)

pictures – and it worked, raising a lot of money for arms and ammunition.

The town's local 'regiment', the 193rd Battery, were among the recipients of gifts from local people, including woollen gloves and socks.

Sweet Melody and its crew of Americans were limping back from Germany on 11 May 1944 without the navigator's oxygen, minus one engine and one bomb bay door. German gunfire did further damage not only to the aircraft but to four crewmen, necessitating a crash landing at Southend. The skill of the B-17 pilots meant that they avoided a concrete ammo building, although they lost their landing gear and ended up on their belly in a ditch. All ten men survived the crash, but at least three needed treatment at Southend Hospital.

The Gas Light and Coke Company, then in York Road, provided a useful aid for civilians and troops alike by installing a wall-mounted cigarette lighter outside the premises when matches were hard to come by.

HMS LEIGH AND HMS WESTCLIFF

HMS *Leigh* became the new name in some circles for that part of the foreshore taken over by the Admiralty. The Thames and Medway Naval Control Service had staff on the pier-head and in the Palace Hotel, moving eventually to offices in Royal Terrace – both locations a matter of yards from the pier. Their role in organising and directing shipping traffic was significant in the war years. HMS *Leigh* was also the base for the signal school, its trainees in private billets.

An area behind the Palace Hotel at the top of Pier Hill was cleared to house the ratings from HMS *Leigh*, and officers too grand for St John's social club could utilise the Grand Pier Hotel (since demolished).

A further part of the seven-mile foreshore was commandeered in 1942 as a shore training and accommodation base, and was given a more widely used name – HMS *Westcliff*. It was officially opened and inspected by Lord Mountbatten, head of Combined Operations, in 1943. This was effectively a land-based naval station consisting of a series of requisitioned dwellings – and nissen huts – along Westcliff and Chalkwell seafront, home to more than 3,000 military personnel. Not only men in transit, but also equipment on the way to North Africa, Italy or Normandy was stored here. Officers were based in the Grosvenor Hotel, and all the other empty hotels in the area were requisitioned. During the war years, as many as 100,000 ratings would have been in and out of HMS *Westcliff* at some point. Many of the town's residents would have been amused at one of Lord Haw Haw's fanciful radio announcements which declared that HMS *Westcliff* had been sunk!

UNEXPECTED CASUALTIES

The blackout took a bit of getting used to. In fact, it seems that the first casualty of the war (September 1939) was twenty-five-year-old Robert Banham, a motorcyclist from Westbourne Grove, who was knocked down and killed by a van driver in Victoria Avenue because he and his bike were rendered invisible in the blackness.

It wasn't just the blackout that was responsible for casualties. On Wednesday, 2 September 1942, three young privates were killed in York Road on an early morning march. They and a dozen others were literally mown down by a Corporation bus in York Road when the fifty-one-year-old driver, Frank Clark from Prittlewell, was temporarily blinded by the sunlight. The dead were trapped under the wheels until the ambulance arrived, and the privates were subsequently named as Ivor Giles, nineteen, Leslie Fairhall, twenty, and Leonard Craine, nineteen, their bodies identified from their Army identity discs and paybooks. Subsequently, Frank Clark was charged with manslaughter, and sentenced to six months in prison.

The following year, the Army became the perpetrators rather than the victims. In July, Gunner Richard Baitey, twenty-nine, from the Royal Artillery, was charged with dangerous driving and manslaughter after his Army lorry had mounted the pavement in York Road (obviously a black spot) and killed seventy-three-year-old Miss Beatrice Minto of Woodgrange Drive and Mrs Laura Clark, an eighty-one-year-old Londoner. Gunner Baitey escaped the manslaughter charge but was found guilty of dangerous driving.

CHAPTER TWO

THE PIER, THE GARRISON, THE AIRPORT

Local rumour had it that if the lights of the pier did not come on, it would be a sign that Chamberlain was about to announce that Britain was indeed at war with Germany. This proved to be true, with no lights visible on Saturday, 2 September 1939 – the announcement, on 'the wireless', followed at 11.15 the next morning. The landmark – officially commandeered by the Navy on 25 August – now took on quite a different role.

Between September 1939 and June 1945, 106,500,000 tons of shipping passed through the Port of London, all of which had to pass Southend pier, which served as a convoy assembly point, controlling all of this shipping. The first convoy of the war sailed from the pier's end on 7 September 1939. It was still open to the public at this stage – for a few more days only.

The first attack on the pier, and perhaps most serious, was on 22 November 1939, but raids continued throughout the war years. Although convoys were regularly delayed by the presence of mines, by the end of the war, nearly 3,500 convoys (with over 84,000 vessels) sailed from Southend in one capacity or another. When one ship with a 'Mohammedan' (Muslim) crew refused to sail on their designated day, a feast day, until they had sacrificed a sheep according to ritual, Naval Control duly secured the sheep from London and sent it aboard in a tug so that the ship could sail on time.

For additional effectiveness, pill-boxes were built and machine gun posts installed with depth charges at the pier-head. Provision for searchlights on the pier had been arranged before the outbreak of hostilities. The structure also boasted a sick bay, post office and its own firemen. A pipe-line one-and-a-half miles long carried over 50,000 tons of water from shore to ship along the pier, and anti-aircraft balloons (known as kites) were prepared on its decks and taken to ships by small craft. The pier had its own defence officer, Lieutenant Commander Whittle, a former Navy diver – and sprinter.

As communication was so important, the telephone switchboard (with 100 extensions) on the pier was manned twenty-four hours per day, and five tele-printers with ten operators worked in watches. An average of 350 signals were dealt with every twenty-four hours.

Greater London, the Southend lifeboat, was stationed at the end of the pier, helping to save ships and to land over 300 rescued crews. The Sun tugs also had a role to play from the pier-head, regularly manoeuvring the ships and towing ones that had broken down or were damaged.

When German air raids commenced, the Army built a special upper deck on the Prince George Extension of the pier and mounted anti-aircraft guns in concrete emplacements. Loud hailers were also installed, powered by electric batteries, so that instructions could be heard by craft some distance away.

Electricians, plumbers, shipwrights and fitters were all on call for ships in need – thousands of batteries for the ships' lighting were re-charged, storm damage was repaired, and guns mounted by pier staff. Not just the Navy, but also the Army, had staff literally living on the pier, with soldiers ready with demolition charges. The RAF were there too, taking on the responsibility of repairing the kite balloons and filling them with gas. By D-Day there was even an American signal station.

A catering contractor (not the NAAFI who could not serve civilians) was kept busy supplying ship and shore from the pier café. Staff there had to contend at one point with fifty ships held up by mines for five days, all of whom had to be supplied with food, not to mention the little ships who called at Southend pier *en route* during Dunkirk. The Ice Cream Soda Parlour, however, had become the pier's operational centre, and the Solarium became the Convoy School – the place where some 3,000 conferences were held.

The train that runs to the end of the pier as a tourist attraction in peacetime was then used to carry over a million servicemen to and from the ships at the pier-head. Food, stores, ammunition and special equipment were also carried back and forth. The electric railway ran day and night, despite enemy action and the regularity of vessels colliding with the lengthy structure. The wounded were brought ashore – some in specially adapted carriages – and the able-bodied were taken to troop ships moored and ready at the end of the pier.

Between June and November 1944, 2,715 wounded were treated on the naval sick bay on the pier, from all the services, including the Merchant Services and the allies.

Yet again, in spite of the bombs dropped in and around Southend, the pier was never hit, although there were a few near misses.

During the Second World War, the garrison was originally occupied by those guarding the artillery-testing site, but later became again a kind of transit camp for others. Such large numbers passed through that wooden huts had to be built on the sports field to extend the available accommodation. Most of its long-term residents were gunner reservists and hundreds of militia were trained on the site.

Although it had escaped attack during the First World War, in the Second World War the garrison was hit on a number of occasions, with 18 August 1940 one of its darkest days (when hundreds of tons of bombs dropped on the New Ranges). The garrison was armed with six-inch naval guns that had a range of seven miles as protection against sea-borne invasion. But the new dangers of air attack – given its proximity to the estuary shipping – meant that the training school was moved this same year to Llandudno.

Experimental work, training, and the development of new weapons continued throughout the war years. As an indicator of the garrison's status, Winston Churchill visited the site several times, the first in 1941 for a rocket demonstration.

One minor revolution was instigated by female corporal Gerry Kelly of the EAGs (Experimental Assistants in Gunnery). The normal uniform included a navy blue skirt and navy pullover, but when she wore the Gunners' battledress – and was put on a charge for wearing inappropriate uniform – the Colonel (Lickman) rather took to the idea. In the end, all EAGs were instructed to wear the more practical battledress.

VE Day at the garrison was celebrated in real style. The garrison was able to show off many weapons previously on the 'secret' list, with the added attraction of a funfair, gymkhana display, cricket match and sideshows. In the evening, dances were held in the camp gymnasium and in the Garrison Theatre.

By 1935, the airport had been reactivated by the council and given a public operations licence, operated by Southend Flying Club. Four years later, it was requisitioned by the Air Ministry and renamed RAF Rochford. The first twelve Spitfires – from 54 Squadron – arrived on 11 August 1939. Hurricanes from 56 Squadron arrived soon after, joined in October by the City of London 600 Squadron equipped with Blenheim night-fighters, pioneering radar operations. The squadrons formed part of the Rochford Line, defending the East Coast convoys and the Thames corridor. Unsurprisingly, residents within 1,000 yards of the airport were ordered to leave, with very little notice. They could take only hand luggage and animals, and had to return for their furniture.

The Heinkel 111 shot down into the sea near Southend was claimed as the first enemy aircraft to be shot down over England – on 20 November 1939. Three Spitfires of 74 Squadron took the credit.

Known as RAF Southend from 1940 (after the Battle of Britain), the airport was a satellite for RAF Hornchurch, the latter retaining overall fighter control. In October that year, ties with Hornchurch were broken as Southend became an independent RAF station. During its Second World War revival, Rochford Airport was the base for fighter squadrons of Spitfires and Hawker Hurricanes, the latter claiming the first enemy aircraft shot down at night by a fighter aircraft. However, it was perhaps the Defiants and the Blenheims which formed the RAF's main initial defence against the Luftwaffe night raiders. The 56 Squadron were also successful, shooting down Messerschmidts raiding Ashford in August 1940 and, after refuelling, taking out another seven over West Mersea, all without loss.

In spite of at least seven anti-aircraft gun sites in the area – giving it its name of 'hell fire corner' – the airport was regarded as vulnerable to attack from paratroops, due to the wide expanses of flat terrain. Its additional defences were two-fold: pill-boxes and people. Around fifty of the former were placed between runways (retractable ones, for obvious reasons), on the perimeter and in surrounding fields – nearly half of which survive in various states of preservation. The underground rooms of battle headquarters remain as do pill-boxes within a wider radius, as at Canewdon (a radar station some four miles away). One of the remaining anti-aircraft gun sites, at Sutton, has been declared a Scheduled Monument, its four concrete gun emplacements saved for posterity.

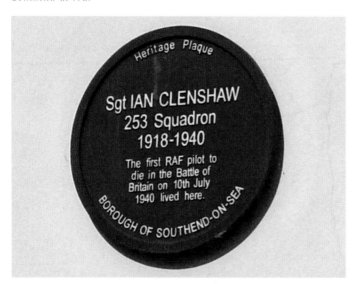

Plaque commemorating
Sergeant Ian Clenshaw.
(Author)

For additional defence, there was a local Home Guard, ARP, WVS, Civil Defence, Auxiliary Fire Service, Parish Invasion Committees, plus fire watchers and ambulance services.

On 18 June 1940, Flight Lieutenant 'Sailor' Malan of Rochford-based 74 Squadron became the first single-seat pilot to shoot down an enemy aircraft at night, and set a further record a week later by becoming the first pilot to bring down two aircraft in one night. The squadron's motto was, appropriately, 'I Fear No Man'.

During the Battle of Britain, squadrons from Hornchurch and North Weald used Rochford as an advance base. Incidentally, the first pilot to die in the 'official' Battle of Britain (10 July 1940) was Sergeant Ian Clenshaw, from Shaftesbury Avenue, who had joined the RAF Volunteer Reserves early in 1939. On the fatal day, twenty-two-year-old Sergeant Clenshaw of 253 Squadron was flying a Hurricane in bad visibility on a dawn patrol, and lost control, crashing on the Humber coast.

Nineteen-year-old pilot, Hugh 'Cocky' Dundas, wrote in his memoir of his approach into the airport on 27 May 1940. He refers to the railway line alongside as an 'obstacle which complicated an approach' and was seemingly unimpressed.

The *Southend Standard* reported an incident in September 1940 where a warning from Canewdon's radar had ensured that all squadrons were airborne when a Luftwaffe dropped its arsenal onto the airfield. A Dornier bomber was shot down at Rochford on the 26 September 1940, and a tiny scrap of this (a field dressing) is on exhibit at the Imperial War Museum, Lambeth.

By 1941, Southend Airport was a hive of industry, because of the amount of aircraft arriving for servicing. On 11 May that year, the airport was bombed by a force of sixteen Messerschmidts, demolishing the operations room and the ambulance garage, and killing one airman. Ground defences shot down at least one raider, which crashed beside the No. 1 hangar.

German Dorniers, two of which were shot down in 1940 and forced to land at Rochford. (Author's collection)

Later in the war, pilots from many overseas squadrons were stationed at the site, including Canadians, South Africans, Americans, Belgians and Czechoslovakians. The latter (313 Squadron) took the risk of being executed as 'Communists' when they returned home after the war.

The 1942 offensive against occupied Europe kept Rochford pilots busy. They took out a munitions train near Flushing (the Netherlands), barges on canals in Bruges, and four enemy aircraft in a Dieppe raid.

One weakness was exploited by a German Dornier in February 1943, when, in bad weather, it managed to shoot up the airfield in spite of the patrolling Spitfires – and escaped. Perhaps this was in revenge for earlier Dorniers brought down in the area, including one which was forced to belly land with a German Major onboard.

The war story of Southend Airport ended in 1946 when the airfield was de-requisitioned. From 1947, civil flying resumed.

CHAPTER THREE

THE ACTION

Air Raids and Damage

On 22 November 1939, the Germans attacked from the air, laying mines in the estuary. Fourteen landed off the Southend coast, with two found in the mud at low water toward Shoeburyness. These mines gave up their secrets once dissected, providing invaluable information which A.P. Herbert, for one (the MP who was a Petty Officer on the pier in wartime), could use to protect the fleet.

Southend became a favourite spot for the Germans to jettison bombs not off-loaded in London. The shipping in the estuary and the airport at Rochford were obvious targets, and the town was too close to both to avoid damage. Another local target – at Leigh-on-Sea – was Johnson and Jago, the boat builders who were working on torpedoes for the Admiralty – although there was, helpfully, an artillery battery nearby, behind Leigh station. Houseboats then in the area were very vulnerable during the war years.

Shops that had basements, which they had been using for storage, opened them up as air-raid shelters during the day – Hiltons, the shoe shop opposite Southend Central station, was one. Public air-raid trenches (commenced in 1938) provided spaces for 2,000 people caught out in a raid away from home. Trenches were also completed in the Sunken Gardens alongside the pier (for pier staff) and in the grounds of Rochford House, adjoining the hospital (for hospital staff). The air-raid shelter at the Elton Laundry in Southchurch had the added bonus of a periscope! Additionally, Anderson shelters were delivered to householders.

One of the first buildings to be bombed (8 June 1940) was Southend High School for Boys, and the first victim was identified in the *Southend Standard* as Robert Barrett, aged fifty-five, the Mayor's chauffeur. A few months later, another incident is recorded (30 August) of a Heinkel bomber being shot down in Lifstan Way by Rochford Spitfires, cheered on by crowds along the seafront. A local bus conductor, John Livermore, was involved in the latter incident – he and his colleagues were on the spot when a German came towards him from the wreckage, with his hands up. It seems that the German

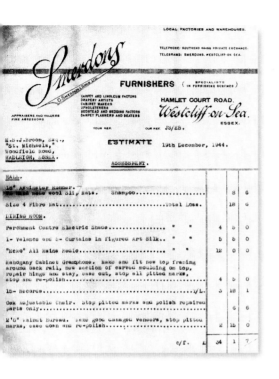

War damage assessment from Smerdons in Hamlet Court Road for a property in Hadleigh. (Shirley Coulson collection)

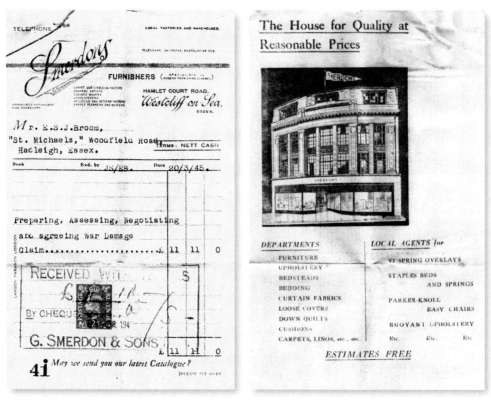

Smerdons' invoice and a Smerdons flyer. (Shirley Coulson collection)

probably mistook the leather strap around John's body for a rifle, although it was part of his conductor's uniform, holding the ticketing machine.

Southend was bombed forty-five times in 1940, with thirty-nine air raids in 1941. One such incident, in the Leigh police archives, involved four bombs exploding (September 1940) in a line along the coast from Leigh Beach to Chalkwell station, meaning the evacuation of the residents of Undercliff Gardens. The Cinder Path and Grand Parade were closed until the area was deemed safe. On the 18th of the same month, a German aircraft was brought down after some civilians outside the Plaza cinema were killed.

There was a serious incident on 4 February 1941 when Southend's London Tavern was bombed, with over a dozen people killed, and more bombs dropped in York Road and Tylers Avenue. Sixteen-year-old Dennis Sutton survived being buried alive for twenty hours at 42 Campbell Road, Westcliff, although his widowed mother and his aunt were killed. The next day, a single German bomber dropped 'a stick of bombs', aiming at the gun site in Belfairs Park. The first bomb landed on what is today the 3rd green of the golf course, with others only yards away, and the account was recorded by Councillor Steve Aylen.

On 26 October 1942, the Luftwaffe raided the town, damaging 100 houses. One German bomber was brought down at Rochford, apparently after an attempt to bomb the

Bomb-damaged R.A. Jones in the High Street. (Ron Flewitt collection)

hospital. The three German airmen were buried at Sutton Road cemetery with a service conducted by an Air Force chaplain, and a squad of twenty airmen with fixed bayonets presented a guard of honour.

In a similar incident just days later, R.A. Jones the jeweller's was among shops in the High Street that were damaged, together with its famous clock. It seems that the fire-fighters had to use municipal drain-clearing machines because the drains were blocked with items of jewellery after this event, with precious stones still apparently turning up at intervals for some years to come.

Edna Glen recalls being caught up in one of the High Street raids shortly after returning from evacuation. She had secured a job in W. Hind's, another jeweller's, and, on hearing the sirens, she and her colleague dived under the counter – which was completely made of glass! Fortunately for them, they were just far enough from Cash Clothing, the store near the railway line which took the brunt of the attack – possibly aimed at the railway line – leaving the whole area shrouded in a dense brown fog. The windows of W. Hind were not so lucky.

Public buildings, inevitably, were caught up in the air raids. The library with its oak panelling, and the assembly hall with its organ, were just two such casualties. Southend

Central railway station had a direct hit in February 1941, damaging railway carriages as well as the premises. The police station then in Alexandra Street was protected by a second brick wall built out onto the pavement, in addition to sandbags to the first-floor level, and police staff wore their gas masks for twenty minutes' 'acclimatisation' every morning when in the building. This was the site chosen for a new 'war room' in 1942, complete with transmitters and a separate control room.

Volunteer fire watchers (male and female) in the town were ready with their tall, domed tin hats and their gas masks to go onto the roofs to assess the fire risk from incendiary bombs – the fires could do as much damage as the impact. Roofs, including those of local churches, were provided with buckets of sand and water. Even the dome of the Kursaal was used as a vantage point, its reflective surface seemingly camouflaged. Other volunteers checked the streets to make sure the blackout rule was being maintained.

People living in Shoeburyness, east of Southend-on-Sea, felt very close to the war zone overhead, with shrapnel falling 'like rain' according to some residents. The battery at nearby Thorpe Bay was one of the busiest in the area.

The Avenue Road Baptist church in Park Street was one of many churches damaged by a bomb (December 1943). Although the roof and stained-glass window were blown to pieces, the church organ survived intact.

The night of 18 February 1944 was arguably one of the town's busiest nights, when droves of Luftwaffe passed over and were turned back by the RAF, jettisoning their incendiary bombs around the river Crouch. The resultant firework display was pretty spectacular – if scary.

The year 1944 was scary for other reasons. Several V1 flying bombs – or doodlebugs – started to appear. When their droning sound stopped and their tail-flames disappeared, anyone below knew they were in trouble as there were just minutes before they dropped, exploding on impact. Three that landed in Thorpe Bay luckily didn't cause any loss of life.

Southend was one of the first towns to experience the additional menace of V2 rockets in the same year (October), which appeared with no warning drone. One of these exploded in the foreshore mud just yards from the pier, scattering hot metal into the town's centre. According to Councillor Aylen, another lifted the hay stack at Belfairs Farm off the ground, and damaged property in Shirley Road, as well as claiming lives. Yet another killed a couple of cows on Two Tree Island, off the Leigh coastline, leaving a huge crater behind.

The 6th Heavy Anti-Aircraft Brigade at Shoeburyness claimed to have shot down some 250 aircraft, including doodlebugs, during the course of the war, not to mention over 94,000 rounds in one month of the Blitz alone. On a happier note, the mobile canteen operated by the British War Relief Society would drive through the town after air raids, dispensing hot, strong tea.

The Southend District was faced with as many as 1,200 air-raid warnings during the war years, with over 12,500 incendiary bombs and more than 750 high explosive bombs doing plenty of damage in the area. The town's grim losses of sixty fatalities by the end of March 1945, with nearly 400 wounded, many seriously, could have been much worse, although this is little consolation to the devastated families.

THE 193RD BATTERY

For a number of years prior to the war, 193rd Anti-Aircraft Battery (part of the 59th Essex Regiment), a territorial unit which started life in a damp shed opposite the Woodcutter's Arms in Eastwood, had been extending its membership with successful recruitment drives. By 1938 they had their own up-market and innovative drill hall in Eastwood Road, Leigh-on-Sea, courtesy of – among others – the 193 CO Major Shenstone (an architect in civilian life), the Ministry of Works and the War Office.

The battery comprised mainly city commuters and was the first dedicated reserve artillery unit, with the latest 4.7in Vickers gun – compared with the more ancient ex-naval guns making up the rest of the area's defences, although later upgraded. Butlers Farm in Hockley and Westcliff High School were used as bases for the waiting 193rd (left and right battery respectively), and both teams, reinforced by other units, were in action when the first Germans appeared overhead in November 1939. This may have conveyed the message that the town was no sitting target – and they have been described as 'the boys who saved Southend'.

Councillor Steve Aylen has written a detailed account of the wartime activities of the 193rd, and the following describes a typical day for a member of the Battery during the early part of the war. Starting at 6 a.m. ...

Southend's Technical College – and at different times the Municipal College and Southend High School for Boys. (Author's collection)

… with an hour physical drill before breakfast. Then a short break; after this … technical classes and drill until the evening. Also, during the day, maintenance and servicing of vehicles and equipment. Two afternoons a week were set aside for sport [and] after every lunch ninety minutes compulsory sport was required [with] evenings spent in debates, mock trials, whist drives and the odd trip to the cinema. This was rounded off with two hours sentry duty, on rotation through the night.

Canon Ellis Gowing of St Mary's Church, Prittlewell, was instrumental in encouraging home comforts for the 193rd. He put out an appeal for footballs, for instance, and persuaded the local cinemas to let in 'our boys' for reduced entry with trucks laid on to take them there. It seems that the battery even had its own magazine, the *Klaxon*, from November.

By February 1940, the left battery was relocated to Ockendon. The guns left Westcliff and, as several members had been learning about radar at Southend's Technical College, they were ready for overseas service. Following a farewell party at the Palace Hotel on the seafront, the men of Southend left Southend Victoria station on 12 April 1940, arriving eventually at Greenock in Scotland, *en route* to the Norwegian fjords and Gibraltar.

SUCCESS IN THE ESTUARY

Heavily armed floating platforms, equipped like ships and resting on circular steel pillars in a cone shape, were towed down river and 'sunk' off Southend (and elsewhere) so that, when connected by steel gangways, they became fortified islands to make life difficult for potential sea-borne invaders. These were the Maunsell Sea Forts, each carrying a crew of ninety.

To demonstrate the strategic importance of Southend's location, a boom was built part of the way across the river at Shoeburyness with a narrow gap left for shipping between it and a similar construction jutting out from the Kent side of the estuary. A submarine net between the two was laid to deny U-boats easy access.

The Royal Naval Patrol Service was equipped for war with ancient guns used during the First World War. Additionally, its trawlers and drifters acted as mine-sweepers, convoy escorts and U-boat hunters.

UNFORTUNATE WATERY EVENTS

An early disaster in the estuary was in September 1939 when the Greek vessel *Parolos* (bound for Greece with a cargo of coal) hit a mine and sank in just ten minutes with most of its lifeboats destroyed. Although three lives were lost, eighteen crew members were rescued safely (four hospitalised locally).

Similarly, some months later, the ships of two coastal convoys ran into a minefield off Southend. Five cargo ships, three carrying coal, were sunk, with the loss of thirty-two crew members.

The remains of the *Richard Montgomery*. (Ian Boyle at www.simplonplc.co.uk)

It was even worse in 1940. On 14 December, for instance, mines resulted in the sinking of seven ships, including a boom trawler and a barrage balloon drifter, although many were rescued by Sun tugs. Five days later, the 8,024-ton tanker *Arinia* (carrying aviation spirit to the Isle of Grain) was mined off Shoeburyness, bursting into flame and resulting in the loss of over sixty lives. Other ships, as the war progressed, had to be rescued on a regular basis.

Well-known aviator, Amy Johnson, responsible for ferrying aircraft from factories to RAF bases as part of the Air Transport Auxiliary, tragically crashed and was lost off Foulness on 5 January 1941. Three days later, one of her Oxford's wings was washed up at Shoeburyness, but her body was never recovered.

The *Richard Montgomery*, loaded with 6,000 tons of explosive stores – mainly aircraft bombs – dragged anchor and ran aground on 20 August 1944. Half of the explosives were successfully moved before the hull split, flooding the holds, meaning the wreck had to be abandoned after a month of salvage operations. The ship should have been on its final voyage from Philadelphia. The hull subsequently broke into two separate parts. (A later enquiry revealed that Captain Wilkin had slept while the vessel drifted towards the sandbanks, unaware of warning sirens from ships nearby.)

On 22 February, 1945, an E-boat sank a large (2,780 ton) coaster – *Goodwood* – off Southend, one of many such sinkings off the coast in what was known as E-boat Alley.

The coastal waters off Southend, its coasters carrying coal (from ports such as Leith in Scotland) destined for London's power stations, became protracted killing grounds during the war years. The Germans recognised the significance of the convoys, of what they were carrying, and used every weapon open to them – mines, bombs and E-boats, much swifter than the coasters and with plenty of torpedoes onboard. If the Germans didn't get them, then the chances were that the perils of travelling in the North Sea – without lights and dangerously close to sandbanks – would; but 100,000 convoys succeeded in their task.

DUNKIRK

When the armada of Little Ships left the Thames Estuary in 1940, civilian boats of all shapes and sizes joined the Royal Navy in one of the greatest rescue attempts of all time, thirty miles across the North Sea. An appeal for help from every available craft included announcements at local cinemas, interrupting the programmes.

This mission to save British and French troops was named 'Operation Dynamo' and took place between 27 May and 4 June, in spite of the proximity of German U-boats and Stuka dive bombers. One such vessel, the Southend lifeboat *Greater London*, manned by a naval crew, saved 200 French soldiers onboard HMS *Kellett* when the warship became entangled in debris, by managing to drag the ship free.

A number of the pleasure boats that served Southenders during peacetime were part of this tremendous flotilla on its way to the evacuation beaches in France: among these, *The Southend Britannia* survived its ordeal. Steamboats were also involved, some succumbing to disaster, like the *Crested Eagle* which was bombed and sank with 300 lives lost. The *Royal Eagle* survived dive-bombing attacks and became an anti-aircraft vessel bringing home some 3,000 servicemen during three trips.

One commercial boat owner in Southend to respond to the call of 'Operation Dynamo' was the Southend Motor Navigation Company (SMNCo). The SMNCo saw that their pleasure boats were adequately fuelled and stocked with provisions and foul-weather gear for the crew, not to mention the essential charts and compasses for such a journey. They were not so happy when told that the Navy was going to commandeer their fleet and put naval crews aboard them, which meant that not only was their means of earning a living at risk, but potentially their capital investment.

Not too surprisingly, given the lack of experience of the naval crew (who could not even distinguish which vessels used diesel and which used petrol), the SMNCo lost its fleet flagship, *The New Prince of Wales*, off La Panne when she drifted (her engines stopped by inappropriate diesel fuelling) inshore with the tide and was shelled and sunk (although reports vary over whether there were survivors). The only vessel returned to the SMNCo after the war was the *Julia Freak* which was renamed *The New Prince of Wales I* and survived a few more years of service in Southend. All in all they lost five vessels including pleasure boat *Princess Maud*.

Another particular boat of local interest at Dunkirk was the *Lady Gay*. This was a motor cruiser built for Lord Dunhill of tobacco fame by the Zabell Brothers in Westcliff, at a cost

The *Julia Freak* (www.
simplonplc.co.uk)

The *Southend Britannia*.
(www.simplonplc.co.uk)

The *Southend Britannia*.
(www.simplonplc.co.uk)

Memorial to the
Renown and crew.
(Author)

of £1,500 in 1934. He handed it over to the Royal Navy as a patrol boat and it proved a
worthy asset to the makeshift fleet, surviving skirmishes around the harbour mole.

Six cockle boats from nearby Leigh-on-Sea – the *Reliant, Renown, Endeavour, Letitia,
Resolute* and *Defender* – also joined the fray, along with many other fishing boats. The
volunteer crews had to report to the pier where naval ratings provided rations and fuel.
These cockle Bawleys were 36ft long, broad-beamed and flat-bottomed, ideal for the
shallow waters off Dunkirk, and also had engines, making them less dependent on sail if
necessary.

The fishermen had no experience of gunfire or naval discipline and most had never
even left the estuary for the open water of the English Channel. However, the regular
crews felt better equipped to look after their craft than, say, naval men – a view which

in most cases had some validity. Although all were under attack from German bombers on their way to Dunkirk, it is said that they ferried as many as 1,000 soldiers per vessel in repeated trips from the beaches to the large trawlers and coasters at anchor in deep water. This strength-sapping activity was carried out in an eight-hour period, in the dark, surrounded by the debris of ships and boats, with fires from burning oil storage tanks. The sea may have been calm, but the conditions were appalling and risky.

On the way home, the *Renown* developed engine problems, and was helped home by the *Letitia*, but the *Renown* was unlucky enough to hit a mine, with all its fishermen losing their lives. The skipper of the *Letitia* (Arthur Dench) could only look on in horror. That night – 31 May – has been described by many as a 'night of hell' with many small vessels left behind in the Dunkirk surf. The *Endeavour*, with a rudder smashed during rescue operations, managed to find a coaster (the *Ben and Lucy*) to tow her to Ramsgate with her load of soldiers. Another local boat, the *Peggy IV*, used on Chalkwell Beach for passenger rides, was not so fortunate, sinking at Dunkirk after a few rescue trips, although seventeen-year-old Stanley Hughes survived. It seems that Stanley was subsequently the proud recipient of a medal from the town of Dunkirk.

There is an interesting story about the *Endeavour*, a week or so before Dunkirk, and not backed by any evidence other than hearsay on quite a grand scale. The story goes that, following a secret meeting in a hut in Belfairs Park, when German paratroops or spies were thought to have landed (the meeting attended by the *Endeavour*'s skipper), the boat went missing and arrived at Ramsgate. There a radio was installed and she was disguised as a French fishing boat, seemingly enabling her to take part in a secret mission where she could collect information on the landing beaches and samples of mines being used.

Many wounded were brought to Southend by local craft, and one resident of York Road recalls survivors laid along the pavements, and of her own house being commandeered by the police to house some of the more seriously wounded until they could be moved to hospital.

It was after Dunkirk that the programme of defence construction around the town was accelerated.

D-DAY

Preparations for D-Day began as early as October 1943, when landing craft were moved down the estuary to strategic points. By February, the British Naval staff at Southend were organising thirty tank-landing ships with the help of the US Navy, with May heralding the beginning of Operation Neptune.

The armada that collected included tankers, colliers, troop transporters, destroyers, cruisers, tugs, hospital ships, water carriers, store ships, in an ever-growing array down the middle of the Thames from Tilbury out into the estuary, waiting for the signal. This force, coded Force L, followed the main assault forces, carrying vital stores and ammunition as well as back-up troops to keep the pressure on the enemy – ably assisted by the Americans.

Leigh-on-Sea was a holding area for the vehicles on their way to the D-Day landings. They had work done to their exhaust systems so that they were above water level, with the addition of a water repellent solution to the engines, and had white stars painted on them surrounded by white circles. Similarly, the car park at the Kursaal was full of vehicles – including tanks and jeeps – being waterproofed. David Knight claims to have spotted at least one German vehicle put into service after being painted khaki, although the majority of vehicles in this locale were British. The main London Road was closed and guarded during the landings as it was full of tanks and lorries parked up and waiting.

By D-Day itself, sections of 'Mulberry' floating harbours had been joined up to make two great temporary harbours, each weighing 750,000 tons, providing an innovative exit route for the swift and successful movement of troops. One section (of 135) passing down river went aground on the edge of the deep channel off Thorpe Bay. This 'caisson', with its back broken, lies on a sandbank, and may be the only surviving example.

The night before D-Day there were over 200 ships in Southend's anchorage, with hundreds more up river. Pilots had to find their appointed and numbered berths among the many, and dozens of small craft were called up to assist in moving the ships into place. The organisation was formidable, with vessels so close together that it was as if you could walk from one to the next. Naval crews had been forbidden to go ashore for a number of days and were relieved – although no doubt apprehensive – when the 507 ships (in ten convoys) set sail from the Thames for Normandy, starting at 2 a.m.

On the morning of 6 June 1944, the estuary was eerily empty, with not a ship to be seen. The town had lost most of its troops, and suddenly everywhere was quiet. Such was the confidence in the D-Day invasion, that tank-traps were removed from areas such as Royal Terrace, Southend, in anticipation.

CHAPTER FOUR

THE PEOPLE

Married women such as Margaret Livermore, evacuated to Ely at the beginning of the war, returned to the town soon after. After having her daughter, Yvonne, in Ely, in 1940, her husband, John, soon joined the RAF, leaving her and her young baby at home in Westcliff's Park Street. She particularly remembers his stint in Iceland, a place with rich pickings it seems because he sent her parcels of material and beautiful shoes for her daughter – white suede and black patent. When he did get home, he was on fire duties and, at the first sight of flames, he was off and running. (She also recalls him travelling from Lanark to London on one occasion in a wartime car with Celia Johnson, the actress, but the details are long forgotten.)

Southend servicemen on leave, 1942. From left to right: Albert 'Ginger' Baldwin (Army) Alfred Wakeling (Navy), Walter Fowler (Merchant Navy) and Tommy Gould (Air Force). (Kelvin Baldwin collection)

THE HOME GUARD

The Home Guard played a prominent role in Southend during the Second World War. Their training included the landing of craft – often utilising fishing vessels – at such landing points as Bell Wharf, Leigh-on-Sea. The Salvation Army Colony at Hadleigh (now a farm) was a training ground for both the Army and some battalions of the Home Guard. Other battalions would have field training in such locations as the meadows on the south side of Lower Road, Hockley, where two nights were spent under canvas. Some officers and NCOs were trained in leadership and battle tactics a little further afield – at Rayleigh.

Greatcoats were provided by the railway companies, and the volunteers had tin helmets from Southend Council's surplus supplies. It is said that the first unit in Britain to go on patrol was at Belfairs: on 3 June 1940. This is where Sergeant Joe Steel, a hairdresser, put the unit through their paces every Sunday. The Home Guard even had its own firing range, opened at Prittlewell in July 1942, and its own band. Southend-on-Sea was part of the 1st Essex Battalion until September 1942 but then became a battalion (16th) in its own right.

Their duties included patrolling the seafront and manning check-points which were located around the town. At these checkpoints, anyone who did not seem to belong in such a prohibited area could be stopped and their documents checked and verified. The Home Guard also manned the machine guns in the pill-boxes when the town was on

Frederick Gale (one from the back, one from the left) and chums in the Home Guard. (Dennis Gale collection)

full alert. There were weapons available, eventually, including tommy guns, automatics and revolvers. Initially, however, Frederick Gale 'made do' with a bacon knife lashed to a broom handle – and he wasn't the only one.

The volunteers progressed to manning multiple rocket launches and crewing the guns of the coastal artillery batteries, even undertaking the specialised and dangerous work of bomb disposal. By October 1944, the area's Home Guard had 4,000 members, shortly before its demise. One local resident, David Clough, remembers the guard room at the gas works, and patrolling the seafront from the pier to Plas Newydd. Such patrols needed two men, in two-hourly stints, one of whom – in the event of 'an invasion' – was to 'hold the enemy' with the ten rounds of ammunition he carried (in his coat pocket!), while the other went for assistance.

Edna Glen's family lived in a house opposite a Home Guard patrol post. As a result, their hall was used to store boxes of ammunition, rifles, and molotov 'bombs', with 'young lads no more than seventeen' collecting what they needed for night patrol and returning them the next morning. Such memories were the stuff of *Dad's Army* of course.

A spin-off of the Home Guard was the Auxiliary Unit which functioned as a guerrilla unit in case of invasion. After Dunkirk, many troops left the area, so the Home Guard felt pretty much 'in charge' until the end of the war.

OTHER DEFENDERS

The local Civil Defence organised air-raid wardens, fire and rescue services, and ambulance and first-aid posts. By 1938, an Air Raid Precautions Officer had been appointed. ARP messengers (and their whistles) were crucial when communications broke down in the town, and teenagers made themselves useful by taking on this role. ARP women were proud of their uniform with jaunty beret, navy jacket with the 'Civil Defence' logo, and navy skirt or trousers.

The local branch of the WVS was formed in July 1939 when 1,650 Southend women volunteered to help the war effort. Their duties involved working in the forces' canteens, comforting and assisting the bombed-out, and laying on local entertainment. They also provided mobile canteens, which were supplied by such organisations as the American Red Cross (three handed over to the Mayor at Porter's, the Mayor's residence, in March 1941) and helped to staff Rest Centres for the homeless, and operated a form of early Citizens' Advice Bureau.

The number of women enrolling in the local WAAF increased to such an extent by 1942 that a senior section officer was brought in to take charge – one Pam Barton, a famous golfer who had won many championships before the war. She is on record as taking part in a golf match at Belfairs Park, a few days before she was killed in action in 1943.

The Stay-Behinds, or Churchill's Underground Army, were small groups of resistance fighters, trained specifically in guerrilla tactics. On the surface, ordinary working men, but men required to know every bridge, hedge, ditch and drainage system that could be used for escape or concealment. The commander of the local unit was the headmaster

WVS honoured at the Palace Hotel. (Councillor S. Aylen collection)

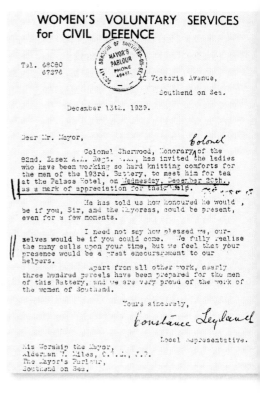

WOMEN'S VOLUNTARY SERVICES for CIVIL DEFENCE

Tel. 68080
67276

Victoria Avenue,
Southend on Sea.

December 13th. 1939.

Dear Mr. Mayor,

Colonel

Colonel Sherwood, Honorary, of the 82nd. Essex A.A. Regt. T.A., has invited the ladies who have been working so hard knitting comforts for the men of the 193rd. Battery, to meet him for tea at the Palace Hotel, on Wednesday, December 20th. as a mark of appreciation for their help.

He has told us how honoured he would be if you, Sir, and the Mayoress, could be present, even for a few moments.

I need not say how pleased we, ourselves would be if you could come. We fully realise the many calls upon your time, but we feel that your presence would be a great encouragement to our helpers.

Apart from all other work, nearly three hundred parcels have been prepared for the men of this Battery, and we are very proud of the work of the women of Southend.

Yours sincerely,

Constance Leyland

Local Representative.

His Worship the Mayor,
Alderman W. Miles, C.B.E., J.P.
The Mayor's Parlour,
Southend on Sea.

WAR WORK

E.K. Cole, the town's biggest employer at the time, was already doing 'secret' war work making radios for tanks, commando packs and aircraft. It was one of the Government's 'essential' factories where radar and communications equipment for bombers was developed and produced, together with walkie-talkies for the Italian and Normandy landings. However, many employees were evacuated to Surrey, Wiltshire or Buckinghamshire once the bombing started in earnest. The only part of the organisation remaining was the Plastics division, which had large moulding presses, too cumbersome to move. By 1942, some war production recommenced in the Priory Crescent works, responsible for such essentials as cable circuits for the Lancaster bombers.

Harold Robinson of Kensington Road was in a reserved occupation during the war, working for the Corporation's Legal Department (then in Clarence Road) disseminating information about – and for – people moving in and out of the town. His wife and two young sons went to stay at Harpenden (Hertfordshire) with relatives, and he recalls returning after a visit there when he was told at Fenchurch Street station on his way back that 'the town had been evacuated' – most people were travelling in the opposite direction! As it happened, there were bombs at Harpenden, too, so his family returned to their Southend home after a year or so. Although they had an Anderson shelter in the garden, he made an indoor shelter for all four of them, which they preferred – and regards himself as having invented the Morrison shelter before Morrison.

Another local resident in a reserved occupation was Ernie Crump, a fireman on the trains from Shoeburyness to Fenchurch Street. Ernie started as an engine cleaner, progressing to fireman during the war years, although he never made the lengthy transition to engine driver, which remained a childhood dream. At one point, during 'Operation Sea-lion', Ernie remembers that the railway staff had to couple together engines and take them to Plaistow and Stratford, away from the dangers of being bombed, but *en route* there were Messerschmidts flying overhead, to the consternation of the railway workers below.

In Princes Street, the steam laundry was at its busiest during the war because of the number of Army uniforms needing to be cleaned. Another switch in output was at George and Son – before the war, they were known for Southend Rock, but turned their attention to producing sweet supplies for the NAAFI.

The editor of the *Southend Standard* and *Southend Pictorial* almost single-handedly produced the town's newspapers. H.O. Crompton did the reporting, photography and the sub-editing for both publications, although the strain was said to have resulted in his early demise.

Southend Central Library in Victoria Avenue (now the town's museum) remained open during the war, with staff sleeping overnight on a rota so they could do fire-watching duty. A lot of servicemen used the library, keeping it busy during the war years – and, according to librarian Doris Patience, some of the maps in the reference library were locked away to 'prevent spies using them'.

Shoeburyness fire brigade, Second World War. A. Crump, second from left, back row. (Ernie Crump collection)

Ernie Crump (indicated by X!) in the Home Guard. (Ernie Crump collection)

One of a number of shops that managed to stay in business throughout the war was Gale's the grocers in West Road, near The Plough. The owner, Frederick Gale, had been worried about the future of the shop when so many people left the town at the beginning of the war, but once they began to return, and with the added advantage of a telephone, he survived wartime deprivation – without even a broken window!

David Clough, living at St James Gardens with his family, worked for E.K. Cole during the day, and did Home Guard duty at night. But in 1943 he went to work at Marconi's in Chelmsford, where they shaped quartz crystals for timepieces and radios. The journey meant a trolleybus to central Southend, the 6.01 train from Southend Victoria station to Shenfield, and another train from there to Chelmsford – plus an extra bus if he was needed at the Baddow site.

A barrage balloon factory on the Southend Arterial Road – Lea Bridge Industries – played an important role during the war. The barrage balloons were used by the D-Day convoys to protect them against dive-bomber attacks while they waited for the signal to depart. They were also used to give aerial protection to disembarking troops on the Normandy beaches. It was one of only two civilian businesses allowed to repair parachutes, and some 381,000 parachutes and 7,000 balloons were manufactured here. The 1,000 workers also produced lifebelts, Mae Wests (life-jackets), inflatable landing craft and inflatable dummy tanks, dinghies and jungle kits which included tent, sleeping bag and raincoat. Even two-man canoes – some of which were used in the Cockleshell Heroes commando raid at Bordeaux after a ninety-five-mile paddle – came out of this busy factory. The downside for its employees, (many of them women) was that they had to travel home on the bus smelling of glue.

Because so many people had left, work was not that difficult to come by. A notice in the window was usually all it took to fill a vacancy, but employers had to compete with each other where wages were concerned because of a general shortage of skilled staff (certainly in the short term) – good news for the workers.

Later in the war, the local workforce was boosted by utilising German POWs. Captured air-crew were employed at Milton Hall brickworks, for example. These men came from a variety of backgrounds – a surveyor, wine merchant and oculist among them.

MORE WORKING GIRLS

The Swallow Raincoat Company took over part of the Kursaal, including its cinema, to make raincoats for the National Fire Service and officers of the various forces, plus trench-coats and other waterproof clothing. The company employed over 100 women, mainly as machinists (cutters were mostly men), and provided music (thanks to the radio), a canteen, and transport for those who had to travel in from outlying areas.

Among the office employees of EKCO who stayed in the town was Gladys Mude, MBE. She was then a shorthand typist, working for the chairman's brother, a man she still recalls clearly – it seems he took the responsibility of providing alcohol for as many colleagues as possible by spending time visiting one off licence after another and buying up as many bottles as he could, bearing in mind the wartime shortages.

Gladys lived at home with her parents in Ronald Park Drive, Westcliff, where she remains to this day – an area which escaped the bomb damage inflicted elsewhere. The nearest incident was at the junction of Fleetwood Avenue and London Road where Westcliff Library has since replaced the bombed-out shops. When not working, Gladys was a singer and pianist and entertained the troops every Sunday at the church services in Southend Hospital, at a time when wards had pianos rather than televisions. Although the area was targeted, Gladys' main reason for heading for the Anderson shelter during raids was not because she felt particularly threatened, but rather because it was shared with the boy next door that she rather fancied!

Modern women now had the opportunity of taking on 'new' jobs in the town – as porters for the LTS Railway stations or as bus conductors for Westcliff Motor Services. A number of women were employed as clerical officers in the confidential printing and typing department at Thames Naval Control in Royal Terrace. These women would have had access to the confidential plans for the D-Day landings weeks in advance, and were locked in 'secret rooms' to ensure their silence. All the instructions for Operation Neptune were prepared by just a few women, who were dealing with the details of beach landings and routing. Staff were ordered to burn all the secret war papers, but some were smuggled out and hidden until the thirty-year ban was lifted.

Land Army girls (3,777 in Essex by the end of 1943) changed hair fashion because for them, and for factory workers, long hair was less practical than short, ousting Veronica Lake styles. Similarly, head-scarves wrapped into turbans became everyday wear after they had been introduced as compulsory in many factories.

Left: Southend Women's War Work Week, September 1941. (*Southend-on-Sea and County Pictorial,* 13 September 1941) *Right:* Land Army poster. (Author's collection)

Girls were billeted throughout Southend, usually in pairs, but worked on the outskirts, hoeing, rhubarb pulling, stacking wheat, potato picking or land draining. On a bigger scale, forty such Land Army girls were housed in a hostel a few miles west of Southend, in Thundersley. They were sent out on local exercises as far afield as the bleak surrounds of Foulness, east of Southend, where they spent time in particularly bad weather digging trenches and drainage pipes to prepare the land for the cultivation of wheat. A working week of fifty hours was not uncommon, even more at harvest time.

Anyone who grew food was also regarded as having a reserved occupation, and this applied to Rhoda Dean and her family who had a smallholding on the Westcliff-on-Sea/ Leigh-on-Sea borders. They grew enough excess fruit and vegetables for their own needs and, her father having a pork butcher's in Leigh, did not even have to manage without meat. This was a busy time for Rhoda and her mother, as her husband and brother were both in the forces (the Royal Army Ordnance Corps and the RAF respectively).

Rhoda drove a Ford 7 cwt van to deliver produce, and took her father to and from his butcher's shop every day, using dipped headlights when necessary. When she had to deliver

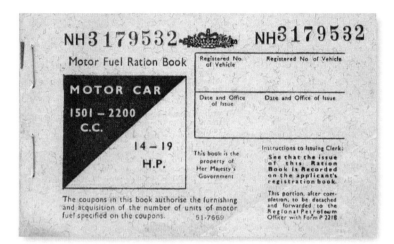

Wartime fuel ration book. (Peter Brown at www.thesoutheastecho.co.uk)

to London, which earned her an extra £1.50, she was always stopped on her return to see what she was carrying into a 'danger' zone – the answer being nothing. No doubt her father would also have been stopped on his way back from a trip to Llandudno where he bought crate-loads of pork fat to turn into lard, but the reaction of the police is not known!

The family also reared hundreds of chickens which were delivered by train from a hatchery in Wickford and cared for in a barn warmed by hurricane lamps, ending up in the butcher's. They had an extra petrol ration because of their tractors and the van, but the farmer in the field next to their five acres still used a horse in his work, and Rhoda recalls him telling her of the day that his horse just would not budge. As this was most unlike the animal, the farmer had called in the Army, who found an unexploded bomb in his field.

SOME LUCKY ESCAPES

The Joscelyne brothers from Leigh-on-Sea must have felt the weight of a guardian angel on their shoulders on 25 May 1940. Harold, Arthur and Vincent reported to the Thames Control Offices at Royal Terrace and were allocated to the cockle boat *Renown*, the doomed vessel that did not return from Dunkirk. However, before their departure there was a change of plan – Harold and Arthur were moved to a sailing barge, and Vincent was transferred to the *Resolute*, which survived the perilous crossings.

The Dalehurst Maternity Nursing Home in Dawlish Drive, Leigh, closed in July 1940 when so many people moved away. Florence Child, the Principal, and Mary Dunsmuir, her business partner, instead decided to accompany children to Australia, sent there by the Children's Overseas Reception Board in part for their own safety. Over 500 people were aboard the RMS *Rangitane* in November 1940 when she was sunk by a German raider near New Zealand. Survivors were eventually rescued by the Australian authorities from the island of Emirau. The two evacuee escorts from Leigh made it back home, having had rather more of an adventure than originally envisaged.

Doing Their Bit for the War Effort

There was plenty that Southenders could do to help the cause: Hamlet Court School could re-vamp men's cast-off suits for evacuees; Rochford Hospital was crying out for blood donors; the WVS Headquarters in Southend wanted aluminium kitchen utensils 'to make into aeroplanes'; and Volunteers were wanted as 'house mothers' to bicycle up and down local roads during an air raid to contact elderly or sick neighbours who might need help.

Because the Southend police – and reserves – were so busy, the Women's Auxiliary Force was formed, and the force expanded into extra accommodation at the Alexandra Street station in 1941.

When the Municipal College reopened, classes were laid on for adults, including 'Wartime Clothing Renovation'. On a similar theme, a Book Recovery and Salvage Drive was held in April 1943 when 107,000 books were donated locally, though some weeding out was done to extract any of value and to donate some to the forces or to local libraries. At the town's High Street store, Keddies, there were demonstrations on how the waste paper could be reused.

Even local dare-devil Tornado Smith, the Kursaal's Wall of Death rider, handed in his motor bike to the Army for training despatch riders.

The Children who Left

The evacuation of children was not compulsory, but some 8,000 (including several hundred from the Municipal College) made for Southend Central station on 2 June 1940 carrying gas masks in a cardboard box and their few belongings, with Paddington Bear-ish identity labels pinned to them. Although a warm day, they had been instructed to wear their winter uniforms, and each school was assigned a letter for the train it would be on: A Train, B Train etc. The trains had sticky tape on the windows in case of bomb blast, and red crosses

First-aiders in Southend.
(Daisy Kebby collection)

on the roofs. Local buses carried the children from school to the station where members of the Education Department were waiting, along with nurses and first-aiders, ready to take an early morning roll call.

The first train-load left the town at 7 a.m., carrying children from Westcliff High School for Boys and Thorpe School to Belper, arriving at 12.10 – a long journey, especially if unprepared with food or drink. The rest (twelve in all) left at half hourly intervals, with the last at 12.35 p.m. carrying Hamstel School students to Ripley, arriving at 6 p.m. Most evacuees from Southend were taken to Derbyshire, Northamptonshire or Nottinghamshire, and none were allowed to take their pets with them, causing sadness in some quarters. Official assurances that the children were well and happy were published in the *Southend Standard* on a regular basis. This was not the end of the evacuation of children from the area, but was certainly the largest and the most highly organised.

Upon arrival, many were met with disorganised chaos. Edna Glen, whose father (William Waskett) was headmaster of the Sacred Heart Primary School, recalls that it took him until 2 a.m. to locate all his students who had arrived at Mansfield – including his daughter. It seems they had literally just been grabbed as they disembarked from the buses!

Some children, although not necessarily ill-treated, were not that happy with their new-found temporary homes. Ten-year-old twins David and Henry Knight walked to Southend East station with their knapsacks to join the other evacuees who ended up in Sutton-in-Ashfield, a little Midlands mining town. No one there was too keen on taking on both boys, and they were the very last 'chosen' by a mining family. The father was in the Army, but there was a teenage daughter and a younger boy, who were not particularly friendly. David can remember 'fighting his corner' on more than one occasion, and he always felt that the evacuees were not welcomed in the town. The one Christmas he spent there was not a happy one, but he was cheered on arriving home to find that his Uncle George, the then Director of Public Cleansing, had collected pieces of shrapnel for him (from Southend High School amongst others) and even a piece of a Dornier 17 which came down at Rochford at the end of August 1940.

Some of the Langley siblings from Farringdon Place (now a car park) were

William Waskett and son Arthur after evacuation: they joined the local Mansfield Home Guard, hence the uniform. (Edna Glen collection)

evacuated to Mansfield, with mum and other siblings moving out to their aunt in Cheshunt (Hertfordshire), but none were particularly happy (especially the Mansfield evacuees). They returned after a matter of months, moving in 1943 to Elmer Avenue to a bigger house, the family having expanded during the war years with extra siblings delivered at regular intervals at Rochford Hospital, Southend's maternity 'arm'.

Brian Yeomanson's younger sister was evacuated from Huntingdon Road to Stockport in 1940, but Brian remained at Thorpe School, Greenways, until the air raids had worsened, at which time he and his mother also made the journey north. After seven months with Mr and Mrs Jones, the family managed to rent a place nearby, hardly seeing their father who worked for the War Damage Commission and spent a lot of time in Scotland. They returned to Southend 'when the doodlebugs started flying overhead' feeling less vulnerable in their Morrison (the Anderson was always full of water) in Southend than in Stockport.

Generally, it seems that inadequate watchdog systems were not always in place for all the evacuees, with locals such as Edna Bright of Rochford never being given a hot meal when at Mansfield Woodhouse, and others being diagnosed as malnourished upon their return to Southend.

THE CHILDREN WHO STAYED

Children's games were affected by what was going on around them. Home-made wooden rifles and bows and arrows for 'fights' were introduced, and boys enjoyed role play – as Tommies rather than Nazis. Children old enough, and responsible enough, became involved in war work. Scouts were trained to assemble gas masks, and assist with sand-bagging windows and doorways, running errands and making tea. Dennis Gale, a Sea Scout, remembers falling down a manhole on to the coal supply for the Palace Hotel when carrying two 'important' brown envelopes. He and his – eventual – delivery (to the end of the pier) were very black on arrival.

Some of the children who stayed at home, who were young enough to regard the events as an 'adventure', spent their days collecting shrapnel and ammunition, oblivious to such inconveniences as blackout curtains or lack of bananas. Wendy Newby remembers being more worried about her dog and the effects of him inhaling gas than inconvenienced by the floorboards being taken up in the kitchen to give the family somewhere to hide in the event of a raid.

A few schools remained open as long as they could, including St Helen's, a Catholic school in Westcliff-on-Sea, although this was damaged by a bomb in December 1943 (luckily when no pupils were there), as was St Bernard's High School (and convent) and Hamlet Court Road School in Westcliff. Southchurch Hall School not only remained open but offered the additional delight of an ARP fire engine in the grounds at one point, and an underground shelter during air raids. There was a trial run teaching children in teachers' homes but this seemed too impractical to continue long term – no doubt to the delight of some. Others realised that their only chance of receiving some level of education was to leave the area once the schools started closing.

Opposing this trend, Bert Callow and his parents and brother moved from Dagenham
during the war years, having already tried smaller rented
and Westcliff. Bert recalls that they had plenty of properties to
ing empty, and were actively – even financially – encouraged to
er was first a conductor and then a driver (on the trolleybuses)
the Kursaal for Swallow Raincoats as a machinist. Bert, although
gh attending Southchurch Hall School, found himself in the
doing the shopping, cooking, cleaning and gardening. For a bit
ied the rabbit cages for the Marshalls who had a newsagent's in
Oblivious to any potential danger, he and his friends favoured
having manoeuvred their way past the barbed wire, and they also
yground which has since been replaced by the Sea Life Centre

at school in Leigh (St Michael's and then West Leigh) during
a different kind of adventure – she was very impressed with
Danescroft Drive. They actually allowed her and her friends
of a tank in the vicinity, with the additional treat of a visit to
ey were treated to jam tart. Muriel Clough's memory of the
of uniforms outside the local cinemas. Living with her family
also recalls her father drawing her attention to the sound of
area, or – more faintly, and only audible in quiet moments and
oint – from the other side of the Channel, in mainland France.
her enjoyed hiding in The Basin – a look-out area near The
eigh – and looking up at the air activity: the British bombers
on their way out to Germany with the later addition of the
as even a relatively good view of the V1 doodlebugs overhead,
ge and the rocket high on their backs (one demolished a house
-Sea). He and his very young pals carved their names in the

n's West Street home (Leigh) was in East Street, and when it
under the large dining table until such time as the Anderson
garden. The family garden was turned into an allotment, with
ds, and not forgetting the chickens and rabbits, the latter likely
her was in a reserved occupation, in charge of the fire station
he car park is now (behind the police station) in Elm Road, so
ily absent was his older brother, who was evacuated to Belper

ol – in North Street – during the war, and the school had
that was turned into a kitchen and dining room after the
was that all the teachers were close to pensionable age, the
involved in war work, but the older teachers commanded
of their age. Wartime experiences had an ongoing effect on
such boys as the Nichols brothers, because Ron – who had also shown a great interest in

the large amounts of river traffic, so visible to the enemy – went to sea as an adult, and his brother, Robert, eventually joined the RAF.

School for Ronald Williams was the Sacred Heart in Windermere Road, which re-opened in 1941 when some of the children had returned to Southend. He later moved to Southchurch Hall School, but remembers having some lessons in private houses. He also remembers that after Southend High School re-opened, only part of the school was operational, so some lessons were taken at Wentworth Road, and some on Saturday mornings (physics or chemistry). Ronald recalls some action in detail – a German Dornier using a machine gun over Southchurch Avenue, a later bomb and an 'aerial torpedo' in the self-same location, and a bomb on the corner of Tylers Avenue which affected The London public house and the 'fifty bob tailors' – what looked like mass carnage turned out to be shop dummies scattered in the surrounding streets. His father, incidentally, worked in Stratford during the day on the railways, and spent his nights as part of the Home Guard at Southend Victoria station, with weekend manoeuvres in Wakering or Barling, complete with camouflage stripes on his face.

Ten-year-old David Knight was living with his family in Beresford Road, near the Kursaal, at the outbreak of war. His dad was a Corporation driver, unfit for military service, who, during the war, was an ARP driver on heavy rescue duties. When David returned, after a year's evacuation, to Southchurch Hall School, his home had an Anderson shelter – which, with earth on top, came in more useful for growing vegetables on its roof than for its intended purpose, although the family also had an allotment near what is now Greenways School.

For David, war was distinguished by his membership of the Air Training Corps. This provided him with a social life at the London Road HQ (with such treats as a billiard table), a uniform (supplied by the Air Ministry), and fed his interest in aircraft and all things allied. As an added bonus, the Corps' instructors – who were given ranks in the Auxiliary Air Force – taught him aircraft recognition, Morse code, and how to play the bugle. The cadets had regular church parades from St Mary's in Prittlewell at the weekends, with banners and drums. These parades included his twin brother, Henry, who played the drum (as did David). David's interest in aircraft and in engineering led to him studying engineering at the Municipal College at Victoria Circus and he went on to join the RAF as an engineer after the war.

As for the girls, the Guide movement came into its own during the war years. There were more than 1,500 Girl Guides in Southend, in spite of the evacuation, working with the ARP and acting as hospital messengers. Older girls – Rangers – assisted the WVS and the Red Cross, and Brownies (aged seven to eleven) also helped out collecting clothes and toys for local children.

Some teenagers, being that bit older, were probably more aware of the danger of their situation, and Ernie Crump remembers being quite terrified when riding his bicycle along Elm Road in Shoeburyness with an enemy aircraft overhead 'within catapulting distance' – at sixteen, he was not afraid to scream out for his mum. Although he volunteered as an ARP messenger boy, his experiences are not at all rose-tinted.

David Knight (bugler one from left) and brother Henry (drummer, second from right) in an ATC parade at Chalkwell Park. (David Knight collection)

ARP and ambulance crews. (Daisy Kebby collection)

STILL TIME FOR FUN...

Although the Kursaal's dance floor was closed during the war, dances were still held around the town – at the Masonic Hall in Southend High Street, the British Legion in Victoria Avenue, and at St Mary's Church hall at Prittlewell. Even the bandstand on the cliffs continued to put on concert parties at every opportunity. Regardless of the size of the venue, a band of some sort was always available, and the dances were well attended by both civilians and troops. The downside for the women was having to dance with men in heavy boots, gas masks on their chests and carrying tin hats. Interestingly, they could have flowers dyed to match their dance dresses by an enterprising florist in Clarence Street (Mrs Swan).

When Frankie Howerd (formerly Howard before a misspelled wartime poster) was stationed as a gunner with the Royal Artillery at Shoeburyness Garrison (later a brigadier), he not only dominated the concert parties at the Garrison Theatre, but took control of a touring party around Southend. The Co-Oddments, as they were called, performed several shows every week, including shows at the Palace Theatre, Westcliff, although Frankie's *double entendres* did get him into trouble (briefly) on occasion, especially with the garrison's padre. A favourite act was to dress up as an ATS girl, along with two comrades, and entertain as Miss Twillow, Miss True and Miss Twist. One of the local ladies he 'borrowed' to play the piano during these years was young Blanche Moore, who went on to be his accompanist for many years after the war.

Similarly, Peggy Mount and her sister Nancy, from Leigh-on-Sea, visited the churches locally and further afield as part of a concert party for the troops. Nancy Mount had her own band, Mountjoy, which performed at such venues as the Grand Hotel, and the sisters arranged concerts for the Wesley Dramatic Society in Leigh.

The Chittock sisters regularly came up on the train from Pitsea on Fridays to join their sister in Southend for a visit to the Regal in Tylers Avenue. The theatre prided itself on live entertainment, and was well attended, the queues outside oblivious to the enemy aircraft overhead. Such acts as Phyllis Dixie (early striptease artiste) and Percy Press (the 'King

of Punch and Judy') featured in the Chittocks' memory, and local papers reveal such shows as 'Meet the Girls' with Hylda Baker, billed (March 1941) as the 'first all woman show'.

Ena Baga, however, the renowned organist who had been playing at her local Catholic Southend church since 1918, escaped the bombing of the London venues where she was playing, and took over from Reginald Dixon in the Tower Ballroom, Blackpool, while he was in the RAF.

Peggy Mount, local entertainer. (Author's collection)

Many cinemas remained open through the war years – even on Christmas Day. In 1939, The Ritz, at the top of Pier Hill, was showing *Wuthering Heights* with Laurence Olivier in October and *Mayerling* with Charles Boyer in November. The Gaumont featured such gems as *Spare a Copper* with George Formby, voted in 1941 as the most popular British star with a greater box office attraction than Bing Crosby. The longest queues during the period were for *Gone with the Wind* with Clark Gable and Vivien Leigh, shown at the Rivoli in November 1942. All these cinemas are now long gone.

For young people, the first youth club in the Borough (The Wesley) was started in Leigh-on-Sea in 1941.

... AND ROMANCE

As for wartime weddings, women such as Doris Patience relied on family donations of clothing coupons – although her father was a grocer and able to accumulate much of the food and drink she needed for her reception at home in Southend in 1943. The alcohol left over from this special day was put to good use on VE Day.

... AND

Postscript: Richard Bunker's mother, living at 32 Sutton Road, received an unexpected letter from the Town Clerk in July 1941. Bearing in mind the noise overhead from both friendly and enemy aircraft, and the noise on the streets from ack-ack guns, air-raid sirens, troops and vehicles ... the letter points out to the unfortunate, and rather deaf, lady that complaints had been received about her 'wireless set' being played in a 'very loud manner' such as to be an annoyance to the neighbours. There is no record of her reply!

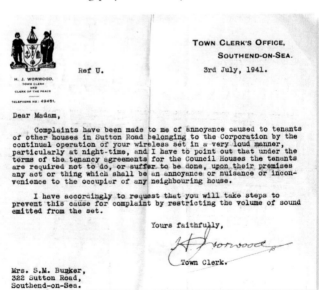

Letter from Southend Council to Mrs Bunker. (Richard Bunker collection)

CHAPTER FIVE

VICTORY

VE Day

On and after 8 May, 1945, street parties took place all over Southend and its environs, with people dancing in the street, and bands playing in popular areas such as the seafront. Some streets erected bonfires with effigies of Hitler on the top, and there was plenty of red, white and blue bunting – and apparel. Huge crowds gathered outside the floodlit Odeon, then in the High Street, to hear the King's speech, which was tannoyed to bystanders while church bells rang out. Even the Scots Guards joined in the celebrations, complete with bagpipes, parading around Warrior Square.

On that day, members of the Home Guard took part in a grand parade from the bottom of the pier along the High Street (much of it already tidied up after the bombings). All the armed forces present were formally 'dismissed' at the top of the High Street, where the Odeon now stands.

Pubs such as the Ivy House brought out buckets of beer for the locals, and an Army lorry from Shoeburyness drove along the seafront with piano and drums on board, followed by singing and dancing crowds. Most pubs ran out of beer before their special extension had expired.

No one was too keen on working that day, which was not a national holiday, so Southend Hospital offered double pay to staff required to remain on duty. The hospital celebrated both VE and VJ Days with services and festivities in the wards and bonfires in the grounds. Another particularly memorable bonfire, for Margaret Livermore at least, was the one outside the Palace Hotel – where all the no-longer-needed furniture and doors (from abandoned billets) were used to boost the flames for several days.

Where schools had stayed open, West Leigh for example, they had their own celebrations, and this school was supplied with ice-cream by a local shop – a treat which some children had never before experienced. The day following VE Day there was a thanksgiving service in Chalkwell Park with a drum and fife band.

The whole town was lit up at night, including the pier and the seafront, in stark contrast to the wartime blackouts. One man happy to see the lights come on was the 'gas man', who could return to lighting the gas lamps in the town, having lost this job for a number of years – although he still travelled around by bicycle, with his ladder under his arm.

On the day after VE Day the blackout was lifted, two weeks after it had been lifted on inland towns. Police cars toured the area announcing the news on loud-hailers.

VJ Day

This may have been celebrated rather more by troops than civilians – certainly there was a lot of partying going on in Shoeburyness Garrison starting on 14 August (the day before) and continuing through to the 16th (VJ Day plus one). The culmination of all this partying was, unfortunately, the death of Sergeant Donald Kirkaldie at the AA gun-site in St Augustine's Avenue on 17 August. Sergeant James McNicol was convicted of, and executed for, the murder of Kirkaldie, following a jealous argument over ATS girl, Jean Neale, although he said there had been no intention of actually killing anyone.

VJ Day was not a holiday for everyone, and certainly not for agricultural workers; Southender David Clough, a member of the Home Guard, spent the day working, supervising a party of schoolchildren on an educational visit to a Great Bentley Farm.

There were opportunities to let your hair down, however – the Palace Hotel was floodlit, and there was a huge fire on Pier Hill with fireworks and bonfires lighting up the sky. Long lines of dancers were doing the Conga around the town, and a few sailors were spotted climbing up lamp-posts. And why not?

Shoebury Garrison. (Drawing by Ernie Crump)

POST WAR

One grim post-war job was allocated to Len Burrows from Ashingdon. As a sergeant in the Honourable Artillery Company stationed in Geel, Belgium, he was in charge of a Grave Concentration Unit, identifying and burying the dead, mainly through their personal effects. Some Belgian families had already buried Allies in their gardens, and were caring for the graves, but these all had to be dug up and re-buried, an upsetting but essential part of the job.

Rather less grim, but still a very sad job, was to assist with the post-war relief of displaced persons from Bergen–Belsen concentration camp. Charles Elman, from Westcliff, was only eighteen when he was sent to Bad Oeynhausen in Germany by the British Army after the war, where he worked as a finance clerk. He was dealing with thousands of Jewish people awaiting passage mainly to Palestine or Switzerland, many of them children. These survivors had put the horrors of the Holocaust behind them.

The Royal Artillery Association (set up in Southend in 1944 fifteen years after Shoeburyness's branch) was one of several local organisations which stepped in to help those who had been seriously disadvantaged by the events of the war. In 1945, for instance, they obtained a grant for furniture for the wife of a gunner who had been a Prisoner of War in Japan, and they bought a pram for another gunner's wife, and a doll for another's daughter. They helped many ex-servicemen to set up their own businesses, and assisted widows and orphans financially.

The year 1945 was also when the last student nurses returned to Southend Hospital, which had served as a training provider for medical students (many from the London Hospital) during the war.

PART THREE: IN LIVING MEMORY

CHAPTER ONE

TWO EVACUEES REMEMBER

Among the thousands of schoolchildren packed onto trains out of Southend was nine-year-old Reg Chapman. He and nineteen other boys from Hamlet Court Road School (now a car park) were destined for Church Broughton, a village not far from Derby. He had been living in Hainault Avenue with his mum, Mabel, who was working in London as a Lyons Nippy.

Hamlet Court Road School evacuees. (Reg Chapman collection)

Once Mabel had said her goodbyes at the station, Reggie became the responsibility of his class teacher Mr Rodgers, from Leigh-on-Sea. The boys were more excited than worried, it seems, although once they had been bussed from Derby to the village hall, they had a nervous wait to be 'chosen'. With gas mask and suitcase in hand, Reggie – and his friend Lennie Fish, also from Hainault Avenue – were chosen by Miss Billings, a spinster who lived with her two farm-hand brothers and teenage nephew in a substantial house with a 100ft garden and an orchard.

This home, which even had electricity, was different to the terraced house with gas mantles that Reggie had left behind. He and Lennie had their own bedrooms, although this was still the era of the outside toilet. This particular WC was, to all intents and purposes, a large shed in the garden with two buckets accessed by two holes in the 'seating' area and pieces of newspaper tied on string, which did the job but also left newspaper print on unsuspecting buttocks. Baths were taken in a tin bath outside the kitchen door on a paved area, with whoever drew the short straw having the last – and coldest and murkiest – turn in the bath water.

The existing village school, for both sexes, was already on the small side, with a curtain down the middle dividing juniors from seniors, and one teacher in each half. So the Southend boys, all around the same age, were housed in a shed with Mr Rodgers, until, once it started leaking in the winter months, they all had to cram into the original building.

Generally, Reg has fond memories of his time with Miss Billings. He particularly enjoyed her Sunday roasts, when fourteen people including nephews and nieces would pile into the large kitchen/diner with its black iron stove. The meal would start (unusually – for an Essex boy) with Yorkshire pudding, the meat and vegetables were fresh local produce, and pudding would often – if he was lucky – be a home-baked jam roly poly, made on a grand scale in view of the number of diners.

Even the memory of a stray German bomb falling close enough to bring down the plaster of his bedroom is looked back upon as 'entertaining'. No one was hurt in the incident, the bomb being meant for industrial Derby, but it was ironic that Mabel Chapman escaped any such close shaves in war-torn Southend.

Because Reg had a reasonable singing voice, Miss Billings, who led quite a religious life, roped him in, perhaps a tad unwillingly, to the church choir. He was then expected to attend morning and evening service as well as Sunday school. But there were plenty of other things he had time to enjoy – the local children, not among those who resented these 'intruders', took them fishing for frogs and tiddlers, and there was an old red model T Ford car in a dilapidated state in a nearby field which became a favourite playground. The boys also helped out on the local farms, cutting hay, feeding the horses, and watching the farmers shoot rabbits once they had trapped them in a confined space. They could also watch the locally formed Home Guard drilling in the village.

A lot of this fun, however, was curtailed when Reg was unfortunate enough to develop scabies and impetigo. This became unpleasant enough for him to have to spend a year in the special hospital set up for evacuees in the local stately home, Barrow Hall, taken over by the council for the duration of the war. The house has since burned down, but was a luxurious building for Reg and other hospitalised boys, with at one point just three

Reggie Chapman (right), Miss Billings and Lennie Fish. (Reg Chapman collection)

of them sharing a huge bedroom with a luxury *en-suite* bathroom, an open fire and a great view of the large gardens. A teacher came into the wards to see their education was uninterrupted, and Reg remembers jigsaw-puzzle afternoons which kept them occupied while stuck in bed. One infection after another made this quite a lengthy stay, although, as his feet (the most affected area) got better, Matron took him away from Barrow Hall on occasion to the cinema. His mother, too, came to visit him during his stay and took him to the cinema, but she lost Miss Billings' umbrella on this visit, resulting in some embarrassment.

The main contact between Reg and his mother were their frequent letters. Mabel kept these in a yellowing bundle until Reg discovered them twenty years ago. Re-reading his experiences from the point of view of a nine-year-old brought many memories back. Here are just some of his schoolboy quotes from affectionate letters which end with 'lots of love' and row upon row of kisses:

It is lovely out hear [*sic*] and I like the school and it is only as big as our classroom.

I am going in for a fancy dress contest. I am billeted across the road from the vicarage where Mr Ro[d]gers is staying.

Our village has one shop which is a post office and sells sweets and toys. P.S. Kiss Peter the cat for me.

Mr Rodgers is going to show us how to play shinty, which is a game something like hockey.

I am going as a Navvy [to the fancy dress contest]. A man I call Will is going to lend me the clothes I will need. After school I play cowboys and Indians.

I got your letter with the comic in it ... did I tell you that I got the 1s 6d you sent me ... tell dad to write me a letter.

From Barrow Hall:

Yesterday when it was cold, our teacher sent us on a cross country run to get us warm. When Auntie Billings came to see me she brought me four new laid eggs.

This time the long line of kisses was followed by the instruction:

One kiss to be taken every hour.

From Barrow Hall:

Mum do not send me any more money as I have been saving up some of the money you have sent me and I have got about ten bob.

From Barrow Hall:

Matron took me to Derby pictures and we saw George Formby in 'South American George', it was ever so funny, and with it was a gangster film that was ever so thrilling.

From Barrow Hall:

Our teacher took us for a walk to see some workmen dredging the River Trent, it is quite near here.

From Barrow Hall:

I have only scars on my feet know [*sic*] so I will soon be seeing you I hope.

His father, another Reg, was on a fishing boat by the name of *Girl Pat*, which had been commissioned by the Navy in the London Dock for mine-sweeping duties. This work, not too far away from home, meant that he could get home to Southend, and Mabel, regularly. Apparently, Reg Senior featured in a booklet published by the Ministry of Information about the different forces and government services.

When Reg was finally deemed fit by Matron, she accompanied him home to Southend during a 1942 blitz. In the meantime, his mother had moved to a bigger semi-detached house in Ambleside Drive, a more modern dwelling with room to take in a lodger or two. This also meant she could give up her London commute and work locally at Garons, the town's biggest catering operation then at Victoria Circus, as a silver service waitress.

His school, Hamlet Court Road, was not operating, so he joined a group of ten children who had lessons in a local house (possibly a teacher's home) until the school reopened later in the war. He took his 11+ in 1943 and moved to Southend High School, only part of which was functioning after being bombed in a direct hit early on in the war.

Back in Southend, Reg joined the Air Training Corps, as he had become interested in aircraft and would, along with other local lads, pedal his bike furiously to any possible crash sites around the town, collecting souvenirs. One (British) aeroplane that crashed off Canvey Island resulted in the ATC boys becoming involved in looking for wreckage, and even bodies, on the beach area.

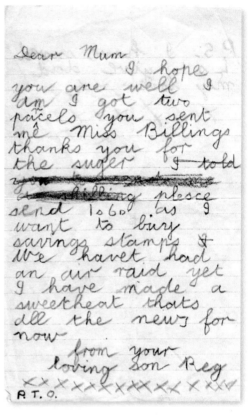

A letter home from Reg. (Reg Chapman collection)

He recalls one aircraft coming down in Hamstel Road, a flying fortress attempting a landing at Rochford Airport. Another memory is of hiding in a doorway at the bottom of Pier Hill to watch the anti-aircraft guns lighting up the daytime sky, starting out at Shoeburyness and then reverberating from the top of the Palace Hotel, the pier, Benfleet Downs, over to Canvey Island with its barrage balloons that stopped many craft in their tracks. Some, of course, were hit and blown up *en route*, and it was all rather like being part of Reg's favourite adventure comics. Even at night, the sound of shrapnel on the roof, the need to use the Morrison shelter, and the glow of the doodlebugs all added to his sense of excitement.

A happy evacuee, and a happy Southender. The bleak side of war and its horrors passed this boy by. The letters, in particular, are a lingering testament of an enriching, rather than a profoundly disturbing, experience. Reg was one of the lucky ones.

Twelve-year-old John Smart was living in Branksome Road, near Southchurch Park, and attending Southend High School for Boys when the June 1940 exodus of schoolchildren began. He had been at the school since it had opened in 1938, and been happy at home – which, although cold, had an indoor bathroom and WC in a downstairs extension which also housed the kitchen. Oddly, the WC had a door to the garden …

It was a bright Sunday morning when he set off on his bike, with his dad cycling alongside, joining the large crowds at Southend station. His upset mum had stayed at home, and his elder sister had a living-in job out of town. The train to Mansfield went via Barking, but there was no change of trains involved, so these trains were obviously 'specials'.

At Mansfield, John was 'chosen' by Mr and Mrs Chell and they walked to the three-bedroom semi, similar to home, where John had his own bedroom. Mr Chell was in a reserved occupation as a mechanic in a stocking factory (which supplied hosiery to women in the forces), but it seems the couple found John a bit odd because he was bookish rather than the 'typical' schoolboy they had perhaps expected. He liked to go to bed early even in the summer to read, and this worried the Chells so such that they reported him to the head of the local school and John was caned for 'misbehaviour'.

The school was the local grammar school in Mansfield which shared its premises with the evacuees – but they were kept quite separate in other ways. Evacuees also had lessons on Saturday mornings to make up for any disruption during the week through having to change classrooms etc. There was less pressure to do homework than John had been used to, which he regards with hindsight as more of a disadvantage than an advantage.

The Chells turned out to be less than ideal as a family for John, and they even went out on Sunday afternoons, locking John out so that he had to fend for himself until they came home. He had been a choirboy when in Southend (at St Luke's) and a Scout, but the Chells were not church-goers, and John was unable to continue these pursuits. Eventually, Mr Chell even smacked John when he had had more than enough of his company and, not surprisingly, he was moved to another 'billet'. This was an ex-miner who ran a small shop, and lived with his married daughter. John was now able to attend Sunday school as the mother in this family was a Methodist.

However, John was still unhappy, as the miner was not the sort who appreciated books or science. He felt that children should leave school at fourteen and get a job, very different thinking to that of John's family. As a result, he was glad of the regular letters from his parents to keep his spirits up. On the whole, the letters were jolly, although there was one letter about three unexploded bombs in the street which meant his parents had to move out for a few days. His mother visited him in the second summer when a group of mothers stayed in a nearby caravan (owned by a family with an evacuee) for a week. John also went home for Christmas, where his mother managed to provide a Christmas dinner in spite of rationing.

Back in Southend, his father, Leonard, was working (for Leswell) as a carpenter, doing a lot of war repair work locally, having been too old and partially deaf (from the First World War) for active service. His mother took a job as a cleaner to pay for the cost of John's keep – because, interestingly, the family, having been assessed, were obliged to contribute around £11 per month, something not often publicised. (John's late wife, incidentally, was not evacuated as she was needed to help to look after her father.) The house in Branksome Road had not changed much, apart from the addition of an Anderson shelter.

When John returned to Southend High School in 1943, it was still not fully functional following earlier bomb damage, so a couple of mornings per week were spent in Wentworth

A surviving Anderson shelter in Prittlewell. (Courtesy of Peter Brown)

High School for Boys in Wentworth Road. He was a bit surprised to see the barbed wire and the tank traps along the seafront, but was less conscious of the bomb damage or the presence of troops. One thing he volunteered for at this stage – perhaps because it earned him money – was fire-watching at the school. The fire-watchers would sleep on camp beds overnight, and were trained by the ARP staff to use a stirrup pump (a contraption shaped like a cylinder with a pump handle on top, squeezing water, rather feebly, out of the attached hose) – although John luckily never experienced an air raid while he was on duty.

By VE Day, John was in Bedfordshire, training for the RAF, which he joined as a 'tradesman' recruit after studying at the Meteorological Office when he left school. This made a difference to his status, and his pay-packet. The day itself turned out to be the day he had to be fitted for new glasses that would fit under his gas mask, so he missed most of the celebrations. For VJ Day, he was nearer home, at RAF Bradwell.

CHAPTER TWO

NEVER TOO YOUNG

Aged fifteen at the outbreak of war, Ron Flewitt was one of many who were too young to be called up, but wanted to serve a useful purpose in the meantime. He left the Municipal College in Victoria Avenue a year early, temporarily abandoning his plans to become a policeman like his father and uncles. Ron's father had earned the French Croix de Guerre during the First World War and taught him that war's system of digging a trench.

As a stop-gap, he secured a civilian job in the police station in Alexandra Street in Southend, one of three boys employed on each shift. Based in the control room and trained on the switchboard, he was required to work either the early, day or night shift, and was in a position to hear about everything going on in the town. The police station was the source of the sirens for the whole borough, while ARP control was in Victoria Avenue (where Civic Centre car park is now).

Billeting arrangements for the Army were controlled in the main by Sergeant Sutton at the police station. Other members of the 'force' at the time were mainly police war reserves, replacing younger men who had been called up. They were an interesting cross-section of backgrounds – one having apparently been a lion tamer. Ron was supplied with a tin helmet with the word 'Police' across the front, but he found this mildly embarrassing

and painted over it … although he would have valued its protection if the Heinkel he saw jettisoning bombs on one occasion had been aiming at the town centre instead of the golf links further east.

Ron Flewitt (centre, one row back) with Southend police force, Alexandra Street, 1943. (Ron Flewitt collection)

Bomb-damaged London Hotel, Tylers Avenue. (www.thesoutheastecho.co.uk)

When off duty, Ron was on his bicycle with other boys, checking out air-raid sites within cycling distance of his home in Bournemouth Park Road. The lads checked out the landing site of any parachutes they saw floating down and took an interest in the vapour trails, distinguishing between those from Spitfires and Messerschmidts. Of the troops billeted around the town, the brigade he particularly remembers – because of their accents – were the 51st Highlanders.

At the age of seventeen, Ron applied to join the Air Force but was still too young, so went to the Romford recruiting centre as soon as he was eighteen. He wanted to be air crew, and had four days of aptitude tests at the RAF station in Cardington near Bedford, ending up with a grading of Pilot/Navigator/Bomber. Although now a member of the volunteer pilot reserve, he still had to wait another year to be called up. He was then sent for further training to South Africa, but the end of the war was in sight (1944) and he was not involved in any active service.

Ron's wife-to-be, Doris, featured in his life during these wartime years. They met at school and studied together at the Municipal College, although Ron modestly claims that Doris was much brighter than he. Because of her outstanding commercial skills – shorthand, typing and book-keeping – she was taken on by a company of chartered accountants in the High Street, early in the war. She was there on the day the London Hotel was blown up, which damaged the building she was in, although she escaped personal injury.

She and her family lived in Sutton Road, near the Starline Paint Factory which was bombed. In spite of such close shaves, Doris was not at all keen on spending time in the Anderson shelter, and was not deterred by an air raid taking place while they watched a film at the Rivoli (now the empty Empire Theatre) in Alexandra Street – although other members of the audience did leave in a hurry. Nor did Doris escape the bombing when she went, with her job, to Bristol for a few days – on the night she stayed there, in 1941, the town was bombed.

E.K. Cole, the local employer, was the destination for a number of women drafted in to take the places of those who had been called up. Doris was put onto the production line here for a while – considered a more important job than the one she had been doing – but, when her administrative skills were recognised, she was moved into the office where she took on such duties as calculating staff bonuses.

For Ron, post-war, his involvement became a different fight: against crime, as he did finally join the local police service.

CHAPTER THREE

A POLICEMAN'S LOT

When Sue Lewsey had the sad task of delving into her mother's paperwork following her death, she didn't expect to find a faded hoard of letters kept since 1940. The letters – scores of them – were written over a three-month period from her father, Sam, at almost daily intervals to his wife, Muriel, during her evacuation to relatives in Northampton.

Sam and Muriel had only been married since 1938, so this was their first separation, and the letters are an interesting mix of tenderness and official-type reporting, perhaps because Sam was a constable in the Southend Borough police force. He had joined up in 1930, and the couple lived in Shoeburyness, a few doors away from his in-laws.

Initially, Sam was pleased that Muriel had left the area, because on 1 September he wrote of 'sirens and raiders' on the very day she left. He refers to a bomber crashing in Liftstan Way, with one crew member baling out over Thorpe Hall Golf Club and one on Thorpe Bay beach, but with three left behind when the plane exploded and caught fire. In this same letter, he also wrote in a

Sue Lewsey in her mum's arms on VE Day. (Sue Lewsey collection)

1. 9. 40.

48, ULSTER AVENUE,
SHOEBURYNESS,
ESSEX.

Dearest Muriel

I got your wire and I was happy to learn that you all arrived safely, as I had been informed of the incidents you had en route. Well dear I am more happier you went away as we had sirens and raiders on that day. A big bomber crashed in Lifstan way 3 were still in the machine but it exploded & caught fire so you can guess what happened to them. 2 baled out I saw one coming down and he landed on Thorpe Hall Golf Course & one I did not see come down on the T. Bay beach. The raid was at pay time, the all clear did not sound until after 6.30 pm. I went to the station but they had gone.

Right: A letter from Sam Hollington to his wife. (Sue Lewsey collection)

Below: Sam Hollington. (Sue Lewsey collection)

postscript of a Messerschmidt shot down off the beach at Shoeburyness 'yesterday evening', with the pilot being taken prisoner; this 'report' was closely followed by 'keep smiling'.

Did Sam think about the effect of his 'reports' on his young (twenty-one-year-old) wife? Although not on active service, he certainly made no bones about being in the firing line.

The very next day, Sam wrote of 'two sirens during two successive nights' while he was sleeping 'at Sergeant Lawrence's', and of 'two alarms already today' with a 'big German bomber brought down' that morning at Rochford and two more down in the sea off Shoeburyness. The postscript, after a row of kisses, reads '£3 enclosed. Just had air raid 4-6.30.'

An all-night fire in nearby Great Wakering is the main subject of a letter the following week. This was the result of a shower of incendiaries…

> … on open land just past the Rose Inn, some fell on a farm in Rebels Lane and the local AFS had a big fire to deal with … water supply was their trouble, a few H.E.s [German bombs particularly prevalent during the Battle of Britain] were dropped but they fell in fields, only casualties were a couple of pigs and some other small livestock.

There are also references in some letters to Muriel's father, who was kept so busy in the Auxiliary Fire Service that there were occasions when leave was cancelled. Life in general was difficult to structure because of the unpredictable nature of the raids – even whether to light a fire was a big decision, because if you lit it, and the siren went off, you would have to leave it.

Another specific incident is mentioned on 16 September when 'yesterday, a big German bomber passed low … with about six Spits [Spitfires] after it' until it was brought down at Foulness. 'A second one appeared going seaward and two Spits were coming inland and … went after him, but I doubt if they caught him … battles were going on everywhere'.

Muriel was not spared too many details in the weeks that followed. On 19 September, Sam wrote:

> We do not get much rest here, they buzz about all day and all night. We had some terrific dog fights yesterday afternoon. Some came down and men baled out, one fell in Burges Road, his 'chute failed to open, he was a Jerry.

He also revealed: 'I don't care what noise goes on if I've got company but when I'm alone I just hate it. I guess I'm scared.' This letter includes a reference to six bombs falling in the vicinity of the Plaza cinema [Southchurch Road] which 'smashed a few houses and shops'.

There is a reference to the couple's second wedding anniversary in his letter of 29 September: 'We will not be able to be together … I think when this lot is over, we can start all over again.' But the war still features prominently:

> We had a noisy night last night and a few bombs were dropped in Southend in the Stadium district [Sutton Road], one dropped on the Starline Works and killed one man … a Southend policeman now in the Guards was killed in an air raid on London.

Although his letter of 8 October refers yet again to the number of sirens (fourteen the previous day: nicknamed 'moaning minnies'), Sam also refers to the difficulties of trying to phone Muriel at Downham.

> It takes hours to get a call through sometimes and I don't want to stand in a call box holding on to a phone while the G.P.O. go half way round the world to get to Downham 82 … if I called from our office … should the siren go … we would have to hang up.

After visiting Muriel in Downham, he wrote on 17 October that he felt he had 'left heaven for hell'. He also points out in some puzzlement that when 'waiting for the bus at Vic [Victoria] Circus, people were standing about talking and laughing as if no war were on.' There is a reference in this letter to 'Keddie's shelter' – Keddie's being the largest department store in Southend High Street.

Another specific incident is detailed in a letter of 18 October:

> We had the usual again last night … one of our A.A. shells came down and dropped in Church Road and killed young Mr Tibbles, the builder's son. This was at about 8.00 p.m. … The most tradgic [sic] part was that he was married and had a young wife and baby and it was an awful job for our Sergeant to go and tell her.

After an affectionate start on 20 October, his letter continues: 'whenever I am alone here I get the wind up. I just cannot help it.' He also mentions that:

> Southend got a packet again yesterday, about eight [bombs] were dropped by a lone raider in Branksome Road and Trinity Road district. Six were D.A. (delayed action) and scores of people have been evacuated from their homes … you can see where the danger is, it is these lone raiders. I do envy your dad [in the A.F.S.] … since I've been back I've been going to the Fire Station more often … all the men are upstairs playing billiards and snooker, some are in their dormitory playing on an accordion, one or two on cornets, believe me they've got quite a band … when I'm there I forget there is a war on. They are all one big happy family.

After visiting London, Sam wrote on 28 October that 'The Southenders are getting like the Londoners in a way, they just take no notice … in London, I was amazed, the sirens wailing and women are still standing about gossiping with babies in prams.'

The letter of 3 November is one of the few that makes a direct reference to his policing role:

> I am now on duty … I have just received a message from Central that the Thames flood warning has sounded. You probably remember me saying that a horn blows at Central when the water reaches a certain mark at the Pier. Central then informs Scotland Yard.

The lack of policing references may have been a security issue of course, although one letter gives an interesting insight into other war work in the vicinity: 'The parachute mines dropped in London that do not explode are brought here and blown up, the noise is terrific. They do three a day according to the tide.'

Soon after (7 November) there is news of a…

… hectic night last night, bombs fell on the mud opposite the Kursaal and at several points around the Borough, but no siren … planes were about all night … Golding [a colleague] sleeps in his house in the passage … I think it best that you stay there because we are getting quite a lot of activity on clear fine days … dog fights all over the sky right above us. The other afternoon, one of ours crashed in the sea opposite the Halfway House [Thorpe Bay]. The air activity seems to increase instead of decreasing.

Quite obviously, Sam is thinking about Muriel's possible return. On 10 November, he writes of Mr Thom's air-raid shelter which is 'quite cosy' with an electric fire and light. 'Well if you do wish to come back, your dad and I have been thinking of getting a fire in your mother's shelter [but] you can still remain there if you wish to.' By now, Sam is getting 'more used' to things and is not 'so miserable' in spite of …

… some excitement the other day, about twenty of their dive bombers attacked a convoy in the river but the A.A. fire was terrific, in fact it frightened people more than the planes, well our fighters shot down fifteen and it was announced last night that the Navy A.A. guns shot down two.

On 12 November he points out that 'the Post Office do their best under the circumstances … I can now realize what delay can be caused by these [air] raids.' Two days later, his letter gives quite a detailed account of 'a big Jerry bomber' which …

… came over fairly low from the Kent direction, he turned left for London … he was followed by about 30 Messers [Messerschmidts] fighters but when they got up to about Leigh a few shells scattered them. Then we saw the big bomber being pursued by our planes towards the sea, our chaps came from nowhere, out of the clouds.

On 17 November, Sam writes to tell Muriel about his visit to the Astoria (later the Odeon in Southend High Street) but makes no reference to the film. Instead, he writes:

… about halfway through our program, the siren sounded. The place was packed and … No one left that I noticed, and it was such a good show that I forgot all about the raid, we came out about 8.30 p.m. … Fellows and girls were strolling about unconcerned at the firing at a flare in the direction of Prittlewell … Suddenly we heard a plane coming in and I saw a crowd of searchlights in the sky in the direction of Shoeburyness and Thorpe Bay, then we heard a whistling sound, everybody waiting for the bus got down low or in doorways. I felt a distant thud … a bomb had been dropped at the junction of the Esplanade and Thorpe Hall.

There is a detailed account (19 November) of bombs dropping ...

> ...on the sea side of the Esplanade about 30yds east of Thorpe Hall Avenue. In all about ten were dropped in a line but not a single casualty. One on Esplanade, two on coke in the gasworks, one near the police box near the Kursaal, one in Burnaby Road, one in Elizabeth Road, one near St Augustine's Church, one near the bandstand, the rest on the mud.

This was one of the last letters before Muriel's return from Northampton. Among many others, there are letters about the glut of tomatoes, supplies of which Sam actually sent off to Northampton, and about some of the dreadful weather conditions prevailing. But these examples give a flavour of the very real danger in the skies above Southend during this early part of the war, and about the difficulties of maintaining a stiff upper lip.

Postscript: Sam survived the war and continued to serve in the police force until 1960.

CHAPTER FOUR

RAF MEETS WREN

When Roy Bunker volunteered for the RAF in February 1939, he didn't know that this would be the beginning of a year's correspondence with the RAF Volunteer Reserve at Westcliff and the Recruiting Centre in Romford – on the subject of his teeth. He failed the first medical, needing extensive dental work, and the correspondence details progress from the results of the medical, to details regarding his treatment, the necessity of a certificate in this regard which went missing, letters regarding appropriate signatures, formal reassurances regarding the completion of treatment, culminating in a letter in January 1940 stating that recruiting had 'been temporarily suspended'. After all that!

Nevertheless, he was finally called up soon after, and has left a bald account of his service as follows:

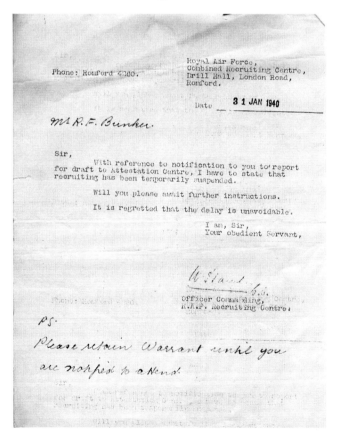

Letter from RAF to Roy Bunker. (Richard Bunker collection)

1940 Called up for service in RAF

1941 Became wireless operator

1942 Became air-gunner

1943 Flew to North Africa – crashed in Algeria – became wireless instructor in Derbyshire

1944 Joined new air crew – flew to France on D-Day – crashed in Derbyshire – dropped supplies to French underground – flew to Arnhem – met my wife Mary at Southend dance

1945 In plane crash in Essex – admitted to RAF Hospital at Ely for six weeks – became engaged to Mary in May, married in August

1946 Demobbed

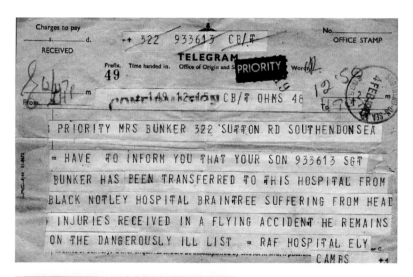

Above: Telegram to Mrs Bunker. (Richard Bunker collection)

Left: Roy Bunker and Mary in uniform. (Richard Bunker collection)

The Bunkers' wedding. (Richard Bunker collection)

At the time of their 1944 meeting, Mary, a WREN, was stationed at HMS *Westcliff*, and Roy and his family were at 322 Sutton Road. The dance where they met was at one of the hotels in Southend, and is memorable for Roy's offer of a 'run home' in the blackout. This turned out to be on the cross bar of his bicycle, a story that became a lifelong standing joke in the family.

   The young couple saw each other as often as their respective duties allowed, each visit from 'Sergeant Bunker' to 'Wren Hutchinson' was preceded by the issue of a Daily Pass, many of which have been retained by their son. Mary, a few years older than Roy, had joined the service in 1944, and became a cook at HMS *Westcliff*. Anyone leaving 'ship' had to leave 'on a liberty boat' – i.e. accompanied – just like anyone onboard a 'real' ship taking shore leave.

Their engagement was on VE Day, and they married the day after VJ Day at St Mary's in Prittlewell. There is an interesting story attached to the wedding dress – it seems that some of the incoming Americans had donated wedding dresses to English war brides, and Mary had gone up to London to choose one such dress – which was 'lost in the post' (or stolen, as was suspected) so she had to make another quick visit at the last minute to choose another. Their wedding reception was at Garon's in Southend, an occasion when Roy had his glass topped up so often that he ordered an over-the-top twenty-five copies of each of the photographer's pictures. This is one reason why so many have survived!

CHAPTER FIVE

ROY ULLYETT'S STORY

At the outbreak of the Second World War, Roy, an established Fleet Street newspaper cartoonist, was at first declared exempt from military service. It was considered he could best help the war effort by keeping readers cheerful with his work, as well as utilising his pen for propaganda.

Although Roy had moved to Westcliff-on-Sea after the First World War, he did rent a bachelor pad in London until after the outbreak of the Second World War because of the demand for his work by the London newspapers – particularly by sports editors. His autobiography, penned jointly with Norman Giller, has many examples of his wartime (and other) cartoons.

A shortage of newsprint and – his speciality – sports activities (including the Football League programme) meant that Roy turned his attention to a daily strip for the *Star* showing how Smith the Brit was dealing with the war. But at the onset of the Blitz, he joined the Queen's Royal Regiment after being told he was 'too old' at twenty-seven to learn to fly, and that his legs were 'too long' for a Spitfire. He only just passed the medical, after living the Fleet Street good life, with the body 'of an ageing man' according to the Army doctor.

Bearing in mind that Roy was, after all, an artist, the Army did not appeal to his artistic temperament, although he passed the officer's exam and was made up to lieutenant. He described his experience as 'robotic and unpalatable'. After a miserable year, he approached his CO about a transfer to the RAF which had now started a recruitment drive to replace pilots lost in the Battle of Britain, opening up their remit for entry into the service.

The CO was sympathetic, realising that Roy was a 'duck out of water', and seemingly influenced by Roy's handle-bar moustache: 'an RAF tash if ever I saw one.' So 1943 saw him undertaking intensive training in Oklahoma as a part of the RAF's Volunteer Reserve. The course, which included commando combat training, was accompanied by an American diet of 'steaks big enough to saddle a horse, and all the fresh vegetables you could eat'. His instructor, Chuck Wood, told him after six months that he was going to pass him, adding, 'It will be interesting to see whether you kill any Krauts before you kill yourself.'

Left: A typical Roy Ullyett cartoon. (Courtesy of Norman Giller)

Right: Pilot Officer Roy Ullyett. (Courtesy of Norman Giller)

    A newly fit and honed Pilot Officer Ullyett sailed back to Britain on the Queen Mary, and was allotted an uneventful posting in Scotland. This involved routine patrols in Hurricanes and Lancasters, and so he managed to prove Chuck Wood wrong. Although Roy played down his contribution in the war, he did point out that he found people 'more eager to laugh and poke fun at life than during peacetime' in spite of rationing and blackouts.

    On being transferred to Harrogate, he met the love of his life, Maggie, a successful fashion buyer. Soon after VE Day Roy was demobilized and returned to the staff of the Star, while continuing to freelance. He and Maggie married in 1945 and settled in Westcliff-on-Sea once their daughter, Freya, was born.

CHAPTER SIX

YOU KNOW WHAT SAILORS ARE

Teenager Eric Lockwood was working at the International Stores off Southend High Street at the outbreak of war. He was a grocery assistant, which also meant that he was called upon to drive the van, or to help out at other branches as staff were called up. On the day war broke out, Eric was in church, and the service was interrupted by an announcement, shortly followed by sirens, although there was no air raid to follow.

He and his family moved soon after from a terraced house in Albany Avenue, Westcliff, to something cheaper in Oakhurst Road, near Prittlewell Station, and Eric feels that they were probably spoilt for choice with so much empty property on the market. Oakhurst Road was his first experience of electricity.

As a driver, Eric remembers the Battle of Britain going on over his head while he was attempting deliveries. At one point, on the road to Brentwood, he abandoned all attempt at decorum and jumped into a ditch until he felt safe. On another occasion, he watched a Spitfire come down in Rayleigh, crashing into a bungalow, and he was one of the helpers on the scene to help the female occupant out to safety.

At nineteen, Eric volunteered, and was called up on his twentieth birthday. The rest of his family had different experiences – his younger brother was evacuated to Burton-on-Trent, his sister stayed in Southend, working for E.K. Cole, his mother stayed at home, and his dad continued to work in London in a warehouse, fire watching when necessary. The stories he had heard from his dad about life in the trenches put him off volunteering for the Army, and Eric did not fancy the idea of being trapped in a submarine or crashing in an aeroplane. As an alternative, he was attracted by the idea of the Royal Naval Patrol Service, which would involve him in mainly inland work: escort duties and mine-sweeping on converted vessels such as fishing trawlers. (Incidentally, this service was known as Harry Tate's Navy, after the pre-war music hall comedian.)

To this end, he went to see the Pier Master, who asked him about his seafaring experience, recruits being mainly fishermen and yachtsmen. Without such a background, Eric admitted only to 'fishing experience' and mentioned a couple of well-known fishing families, and this seemed to do the trick. He heard of his acceptance a few months later

Left: Eric Lockwood in uniform. (Eric Lockwood collection)

Right: Wedding day for Eric Lockwood and Queenie. (Eric Lockwood collection)

and had to go to the Lowestoft HQ for his medical and basic training. Within a fortnight, Eric was on a boat on the Thames in London.

Most of the small boats plying the Thames, mine-watching during the air raids, were converted luxury cruisers, commandeered by the naval services, with a Petty Officer, an engineer and two seamen. On Eric's day off, he got the train to Southend to visit his family, but as the war progressed, and he was sent further and further afield, he got home far less often. After twelve months in the London area, he spent time in Lowestoft, and then spent a couple of years in the Atlantic, off Ireland, in a specially-built wooden minesweeper with a crew of twenty, on the hunt for magnetic mines.

Working in the Atlantic sea-lanes was hard work in rough seas. The vessel used trawling nets with electrodes, which had to be reeled in onto a very big wheel, which needed so much effort, Eric developed a hernia. He then returned to the *Europa* (the naval base at Lowestoft) for lighter duties, but not for long. Next stop was Aden, in very different sun-baked temperatures. The vessel here was an old converted trawler, with the fishing hold turned into living accommodation, which had to be loaded up with coal, regardless of the heat. By now, Eric had passed the tests he needed to become a leading seaman.

Eric Lockwood and other members of Southend's wartime Salvation Army Band. (Eric Lockwood collection)

Towards the end of the European war, the Navy were heading towards Japan, and stopping off at Aden for revictualling. Anyone with grocery or warehouse experience could apply for the NAAFI, and Eric was taken on and went ashore as an Assistant Canteen Manager in Aden. He was now a Petty Officer until being sent home in June 1946 after the ships stopped calling (following VJ Day).

When Eric did manage to fit in visits to Southend, one leave saw him marrying childhood sweetheart, Queenie, in 1943. The ceremony was at the Salvation Army citadel in Clarence Road, and resulted in the bonus of a marriage allowance. Queenie was in the Salvation Army choir, and Eric played the euphonium. They lived in rented rooms in Westcliff, but Queenie spent some time with family in Kent in 1944 following the birth of their daughter in August.

So Eric's war ended with a wife, baby, new home – and a suntan. It could have been so much worse.

CHAPTER SEVEN

PAT GOLLIN

In 1939, Pat was sixteen, living in Oakhurst Road with her younger sister and her parents. On the very day that war broke out, the family had planned a holiday to Cornwall, but quickly changed their plans and ended up at Bradwell-on-Sea.

It was, perhaps predictably, at E.K. Cole that Pat started working (with slide rules) although she had trained as a shorthand-typist, but in 1940 the family put their furniture into store and went to Kent, having watched other families leaving the town with prams loaded with possessions, for all the world like refugees. Pat's sister had already been evacuated. Although Pat found a job – in the Royal Arsenal – this turned out to be a risky choice, and it was soon bombed. This prompted a return to Southend, where Pat watched a dogfight over the pier on her first weekend home.

Now in rented accommodation in Edith Road, Pat became a telephonist at the Southend Exchange opposite The Cricketers in London Road, and worked there from the end of 1940 until 1948. During the war years, the operators were busy passing on air-raid warnings to the hospital, police, council, and to such vulnerable sites as E.K. Cole. Code yellow meant that aircraft were leaving Germany, green indicated that they were over the Channel, and red that they were overhead.

The exchange was actually hit when Pat was on night duty, but the only damage seems to have been to one of the clocks. If she wasn't on night duty, she would have been involved in fire-fighting overnight – which paid an extra half a crown. As many as sixty people worked alongside Pat, plus eight supervisors, and it was a very noisy, lively place, with switchboards along the walls, and a directory-enquiry desk in the middle which needed specially-trained operators. Pat still has her wartime headset, No. 65, and remembers that only those who shouted loud enough and long enough would be able to get a free line. The staff at the exchange, together with the Post Office engineers, became like a second family.

At lunchtimes, the staff mainly utilised the adjacent Bob's Café, although they had their own kitchen. As they only had a half hour for lunch and a quarter hour for breaks, it was quicker to telephone ahead so the bread-and-dripping (the favourite, at 1d, with competition for the 'brown bits') would be ready and waiting.

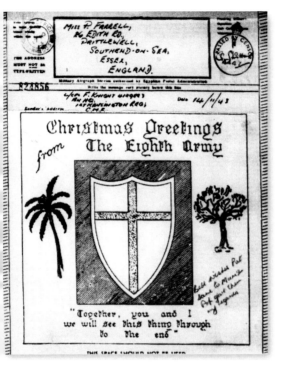

Christmas cards sent to Pat Gollin during the Second World War. (Pat Gollin collection)

Like so many civilians, Pat took the disruption and danger in her stride. During the day, it meant diving into a doorway to avoid shrapnel raining down, and at night, she felt no fear walking down London Road at midnight. When confronted with bandaged and bedraggled soldiers – of any nationality – in the street, Pat and her mother would open up the local church hall (at St Mary's) and feed them bread and milk until the Army came to collect them. More daunting were the dances at Southend Hospital, as it seems the young doctors did like a drink or two …

'Pop' was Manager of the Maypole at 152 Southend High Street, a grocery shop that stayed open throughout the war. His main wartime activity was to organise entertainment for the troops at St Mary's Church hall (Prittlewell), ably assisted by his wife, known as 'Mop'. There were two weekly whist drives, when civilians paid 1s 3d and soldiers paid 3d, with tea and sandwiches provided, and there were weekly dances (same cost) with concert parties, including such notables as Billy Cotton's brother Norman, billeted locally. Popular acts varied from an RAF band to 'Mr Tuthill's Grotesque Shadowgraph' to especially, The Co-Odments, featuring Frankie Howerd from Shoeburyness Garrison, who became a friend of Pat's father, joining them for Sunday dinners.

Every Christmas Day, Boxing Day and New Year during the war, there were parties at St Mary's, utilising the spacious canteen and recreation room, splendidly decorated for these occasions. George Farrell (Pat's father) made sure that everyone (as many as 150 troops) had one of the presents donated by local businesses. He was described in *St Mary's Magazine*

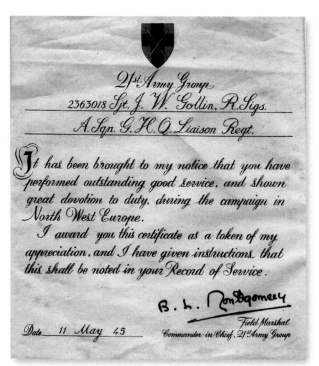

John Gollin's wartime certificate.
(Pat Gollin collection)

(early 1943) as combining 'as many offices as Pooh-Bah, being secretary, treasurer, organiser and general man of all work'. Even the female canteen workers were not forgotten at such times, with, for example, a 'box of powder' for each one at the 1942 Christmas Party.

Pop was also Church Warden at St Mary's during the war, with a 5.30 and 7 o'clock service on Sundays. Although Pat usually attended the 7 o'clock service, she did choose the bandstand with a boyfriend one day in preference, and pretended she'd been to the 5.30 session – but didn't get away with it.

Not surprisingly, Pat chose St Mary's for her own twenty-first birthday celebrations, on the verge of VE Day. This was around the time the family moved to Victoria Avenue.

Incidentally, her future husband, John, a PO engineer from Pall Mall in Leigh-on-Sea, (they met in 1946) spent his war in the Phantom Regiment. This was an elite squad attached to the Royal Corps of Signals which included David Niven and two of Lady Astor's sons, a squad which preceded the main body of troops to reconnoitre occupied areas.

CHAPTER EIGHT

DAISY KEBBY

Bombs dropping in Hobleythick Lane came as a shock after the phoney war for Daisy and her husband, Sidney. Although the area was promptly evacuated, Sidney was in a reserved occupation at the electricity offices near Nazareth House in central Southend.

Above: Daisy's sister Joan in the RAF. (Daisy Kebby collection)

Right: Daisy's sister Maud in the fire service. (Daisy Kebby collection)

Left: The Scarborough Drive bungalow in the 1940s. (Daisy Kebby collection)

Right: Southend ambulance crew. (Daisy Kebby collection)

When volunteers were needed, pre-war, Daisy joined the Civil Defence as a nurse, following some first-aid training. Eastwood School was the base for such training (which included picking up 'bodies' from local fields) and also for the local fire unit. To get to training once blackout had come into force, Daisy rode her bicycle with no lights, but escaped misadventure. Sidney, too, trained in first-aid.

Daisy's sister, Maud, went into the fire service, with another sister, Joan, joining the RAF, where she met her husband – who came from Glendale Gardens, Leigh-on-Sea! Remaining sisters Vera and Ethel worked in London, managing to spend some time with their mother at the family home in 'Yewfield', Park Lane, Southend, during the war years. Although Daisy's mother was evacuated to Leytonstone in East London, the bombing was worse there than at home, and she didn't stay.

After training, Daisy went to the cottage hospital, then in Warrior Square, Southend. There, she took on such duties as bathing local children with infectious rashes, children who were often in dire need of a bath, and were eventually sent home with clean clothes in the hope that they would not return. This hospital was more like a clinic than a hospital, treating the civilian population.

Daisy's marital bungalow in Wells Avenue, near the airport, was taken over by the RAF, although the forces did pay a nominal rent for its use. The building – which they bought originally for £500 – is now a private air club. As for the Kebbies, they had quite a choice of empty houses in the Southend area, thanks to the town's evacuation. They turned down one property in Vernon Drive – luckily, as it transpired, because this was later bombed. Instead, they rented a bungalow in Scarborough Drive, applying to buy after the war.

Daisy was soon drafted to work at Southend General as a nursing auxiliary. The nurses were very much in charge and did not take kindly to the auxiliaries, regarding them as amateurs. Her duties were menial, but, like the nurses, the auxiliaries had to contend with criticism from the matron, who noticed every bit of fluff left around the bed wheels. The Warrior Square hospital became a depot for the mobile ambulance service.

As a vegetarian, Daisy had an extra cheese ration instead of her meat allowance, and used her ration coupons at the health food store in Leigh Road. Her extra cheese was envied by some, it seems. Food was generally not that expensive because shops had fewer customers. It was even possible to pick fruit and flowers from abandoned gardens! Even holidays were managed on occasion during the war years – to Worthing on the South coast, considered a safe area, with her older sister-in-law and family. Something else that was perhaps a little unusual in those years was the sale of the Wells Avenue bungalow to a Warrior Square agent called Albrecht. It was sold for £650, securing around £150 profit – quite a bonus just when funds were needed.

Daisy recalls standing on the cliffs at the bottom of Avenue Road watching the boats stockpiling in preparation for Dunkirk. Some time later, she and Maud watched a parachute floating down, which seems to have ended up somewhere around the West Leigh Schools area. As for the many troops billeted in the town, it is the wolf-whistles that persist in Daisy's memory rather than anything darker. So, while life went on, the war was very much all around. Another reminder was the necessity for London relatives to acquire a special 'pass' if they wanted to visit Southend.

In 1941, Sidney's occupation was re-prioritised and no longer 'reserved', so he volunteered for the Royal Electrical and Mechanical Engineers, rather than be foisted into something not of his choosing. Although doing mainly clerical work, he had to learn to drive a HGV lorry and was part of a convoy which went over to France. He ended up in Belgium, staying on to do engineering work on the vehicles there.

When Christine was born in 1943, Sidney was in Ashford, and got limited compassionate leave to be with his new daughter. Christine was born at home, a midwife in attendance, on the very night a bomb was dropped at Jones' Corner.

Daisy and Sidney in uniform. (Daisy Kebby collection)

Above: Protected from gas, and the rest! (Daisy Kebby collection)

Left: Christine Kebby in the pram. (Daisy Kebby collection)

The post-birth procedure then was for mothers to stay in bed for twelve days. Although someone should have moved in after the birth, Daisy was let down. Luckily, her sister was on hand, able to bring trays of food. After ten days, Daisy ventured into her drive, to the consternation of the neighbours!

Once she had Christine to care for, Daisy stayed at home, but she was content to do so – although she had enjoyed the camaraderie and the job. It didn't matter that her home was cold and damp; and she shared Sidney's pride in his roses. The large pram she bought to push Christine around was a second-hand buy, as were many of her possessions.

Where rationing was concerned, its biggest impact on Daisy was the lack of bananas. When some foods – including bananas – became available if you were prepared to queue, she and her sister Vera did just that so they could make banana sandwiches as a treat for Vera's children, and Christine. However, to their great disappointment, the children didn't like them at all, thinking they had a very strange taste.

CHAPTER NINE

WENDY NEWBY

Before the war, Wendy had been living with her parents and sister in Cranleigh Avenue, Westcliff-on-Sea, but her father removed the family – including aunts and nieces – to Henley-on-Thames, further from the action. However, by 1944, Wendy (at seventeen and a half) had joined the Army, following in her sister's footsteps. Both of them ended up back 'home' – at Shoeburyness Garrison.

Lance Corporal Mary Newby was a shorthand-typist at the garrison, and Wendy was a messing clerk, preparing all the catering figures. The sisters slept in separate nissen huts, each shared with about seven girls, in Wakering Road, with the sound of shrapnel falling on the metal roof. These temporary abodes – one of which housed the canteen – were not exactly 'safe' as they were located in a field adjacent to an underground ammunition dump.

Doodlebugs became a common occurrence, but the most memorable cut out above the treetops when Wendy was carrying a pile of ironing. In an attempt to save herself, if not the ironing, Wendy put it on her head and dived to the ground – and the doodlebug did a U-turn and went out to sea, suggesting that the 'cut out' mechanism was – thankfully – faulty. Another near miss found her in the office on the second floor of the 'Manor House' in the garrison, opposite 'A' Battery, who set off a device which blew her across the room.

Wendy became a lance corporal by the time her sister was demobbed, and her fondest memories are of i) meeting her husband who visited the garrison and ii) VE Day. The latter was announced with the sound of the plating bell on the range, which rang late in the evening. All the girls put trousers over their pyjamas and went to wake anyone still (surprisingly) asleep, creating havoc in their wake, surmounted only by the celebrations in Civvy Street – even pianos were dragged out of houses. Wendy spent the rest of that memorable day writing out leave passes. As she says, someone had to do it. And it was the best job she'd had 'all war'.

CHAPTER TEN

PAT P.

Living in the Ridgeway, Pat qualified as a ballet teacher at the outbreak of war, but now joined her mother in the WVS. She found this to be quite a culture shock. The two women were sent to the technical college in Southend to make camouflage nets using an array of different coloured canvases. The dye stuck to her skin and her clothes, the work was fiddly, the canvases were grubby, and the place was crowded and noisy, with a lot of women working on huge tables.

Pat then tried the Civil Defence in the ARP control centre in Victoria Avenue, not far from where the police station is now. This was a little better, because she was answering telephones, sending out rescue calls from the air-raid wardens, and keeping a record of raids on a large wall map. Each worker here had their own private 'cubicle', but Pat didn't like the shift work and nor did she like the metal bunks they used for 'rest' when working at night.

More happily, Pat got engaged in 1940 and married her childhood sweetheart in 1941. The arrangements had been made in a hurry to suit his leave from his interpreting work with the Free French Forces in London, and she'd received a telegram saying 'LEAVE GRANTED STOP HOME WEDNESDAY STOP WEDDING FRIDAY STOP'.

The wedding took place at St Helen's Church in Milton Road, with a Spam wedding breakfast at the Palace Hotel. Because of the rationing in force, wedding cake was not readily available, and Pat declined an offer of a cardboard replica! It seems that lace was not rationed, however, and Pat's mother found some blue lace in a London store that was made up into a wedding dress. Their five-day honeymoon was at a hotel in Richmond Hill, with a trip to see the Crazy Gang on stage in London.

CHAPTER ELEVEN

CELIA WALDMAN

Thorpe Bay retiree, Celia Waldman, was one of that famous band of women who stepped in to fill the breaches left by farm workers who were busy defending their country: The Land Army. Originally from East Ham, Celia, at seventeen, liked the idea of joining the Army, but her mother was not keen, as she had lost a son early in the war.

They settled on the Land Army, and young Celia reported to the purpose-built Land Army hostel at Thundersley, just outside Southend. Her uniform included breeches, a tan overcoat, hat, and very uncomfortable lace-up brogues which later gave her all sorts of problems with her feet.

The Thundersley hostel was a kind of training set-up for around fifty girls from all over the country, who slept in bunks in dormitories. In the morning, after breakfast, they had their instructions for the day, and a lorry would arrive to take small groups to different destinations around the fringes of Southend. Their duties focused on clearance and cutting down trees, but encompassed every kind of farm work. During her six months here in 1941, Celia remembers one girl meeting a Polish soldier and leaving to get married.

Celia Waldman, a Land Army girl. (Celia Waldman collection)

Celia and sheepdog on duty. (Celia Waldman collection)

After this initial training, she and another recruit (Doreen, widowed at a young age when her husband died in service with the RAF) were billeted to the Gregs' farmhouse in Wakering. They had their own bedroom, converted from an extra sitting room, and all the food they could eat from the farm, which was very self sufficient. Although there was no electricity, Mr Greg had his own generator on the sea-wall, and there was Calor gas for cooking. There was the luxury of a bathroom, and a telephone so they could keep in touch with their families. They were treated very well – Mrs Greg even did their washing – and were paid 10s per week, although they had to buy their own bicycles.

The bicycles were essential because every day they 'commuted' from the Wakering house to the Gregs' farmland on Potton Island (a few miles north of Southend) on unmade roads, starting around 7.30 in the morning until it was time for their evening meal. They took their own lunches to eat in the open air. Very occasionally, they had to row across if they misjudged the tide. The island was a peaceful haven, in spite of the activity in the skies above, and boasted just three cottages – the two girls could spend a day working and not see a soul. A great place to get a suntan in the summer, but raw and difficult during the winter months.

The girls' duties were diverse, and they accumulated a number of extra skills – how to drive mechanised tractors and threshers, how to milk a cow and even castrate a calf. One day a barrel of molasses being ferried by horse-and-cart went over a bump, one barrel landing on Celia's already sore feet, damaging a couple of toes permanently. (This resulted in a visit to the Elizabeth Garrett Anderson Hospital in London for treatment, mainly a gynaecological hospital, to the naïve Celia's embarrassment.)

Additionally, Celia and Doreen had to be there when cattle arrived at Shoeburyness station by train, and, with the help of the farmer's sheepdogs, walk the animals to the island – or walk others back who were ready for the slaughterhouse. This always attracted amused attention from the locals, but was not an easy task.

During their limited time off, the girls could visit Southend and Celia remembers shopping at Keddies and at Garon's with the little cash they had to spare. Socially, Southend was full of pubs and troops, so Celia was not short of male company. A different kind of male company arrived towards the end of the war – prisoners of war. The first to arrive were Italians, friendly and flattering, one of whom made Celia a charming cigarette case, still in her possession. Then came the Germans, rather more sullen. These men were dropped off by lorries, often with little knowledge of the language, but farming is a universal skill and, during harvests, they provided welcome assistance.

This was probably the closest to a safe haven during the war that you could get locally, while still feeling that you were 'doing your bit'.

Above: The cigarette case made by an Italian POW. (Celia Waldman collection)

Right: Belated recognition – 2008 Land Army certificate. (Celia Waldman collection)

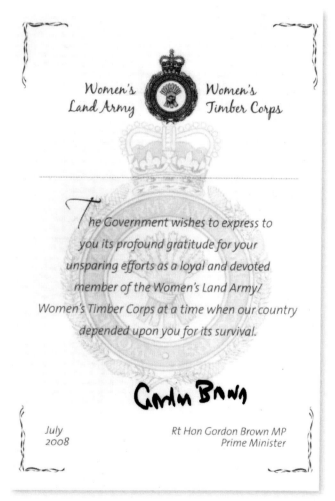

Women's Land Army   Women's Timber Corps

The Government wishes to express to you its profound gratitude for your unsparing efforts as a loyal and devoted member of the Women's Land Army/ Women's Timber Corps at a time when our country depended upon you for its survival.

Gordon Brown

July 2008

Rt Hon Gordon Brown MP
Prime Minister

CHAPTER TWELVE

BARBARA CROWE – IN HER OWN WORDS

My grandparents, aunts, uncles and cousins all lived in the East End, but the two elder sisters of my maternal grandmother had retired from being East End pub licensees and had bought houses in Westcliff-on-Sea. Pre-war we had visited Westcliff on several occasions, and one of the great-aunts suggested to my parents that we go to stay with her to help us recover from the whooping cough[1]. So we came to stay in the Victorian house in Westcliff in which my husband and I have since lived for the fifty-two years of our married life.

Our stay in Westcliff was initially meant to be temporary, to help my sister and me recover from our illness ... My other great-aunt ... had returned to live with my grandmother in London. She had tenants in her Westcliff house who suddenly decided to move and so she offered that house to my parents. My father had to apply to Southend Council for permission to move into the area and I found a letter in his papers after his death, from the council, intimating that we could move in because of our circumstances, but in future the town would be closed to newcomers ...

There were some bombs in the town which caused considerable damage, including one near St Bernard's Convent which was at the end of my great-aunt's road and caused much glass to be broken in her house and others, and a great deal of damage to Avenue Baptist Church. However, compared to London we found it peaceful.

As far as schooling was concerned, I was now seven and had as yet had little formal teaching. My parents found that Hamlet Court School would take me, but much of the school beside the London Road had been bombed and was unusable, so the small number of children in the area shared the infant block situated by Claremont Road ...

My time at Hamlet Court School was very happy, with good dedicated teachers. On odd occasions the air-raid warning would go off and we would go into the brick-built shelters in the playground, but only once can I remember hearing a bomb explode and that was when Jones, the jeweller's in the High Street, received a direct hit and a considerable number of other shops were badly damaged. In 1944 part of the main school building was

1 Note, not to escape the bombing! – *Author*

Barbara Crowe (*née* Greenland, far left) and the Victory Kids. (Barbara Crowe collection)

rebuilt and I remember being asked by my teacher, Miss East, to help her move equipment in to the restored building – and with great excitement our class moved in.

My memories of those years were mainly happy with, surprisingly, considering it was wartime, a sense of freedom. We walked to school on our own, going home for lunch and the only time Mum accompanied me was on Friday afternoons so that I could spend my sweet ration for the week – one Fry's chocolate bar was usually my choice.

We played out in the streets with our friends with no thought of danger. I enjoyed Brownies and Sunday School and the occasional trip to London for special family events. On 24 May each year we celebrated Empire Day and at school we dressed for the day in the uniform of the particular organisation we belonged to, such as Brownies, Guides, Cubs and Scouts etc. We performed country dances in the playground and sang 'I Vow to Thee my Country'. The feeling of patriotism in those days of war was inevitably very strong …

My real sadness was the loss of a much-loved baby brother, born to my parents when they came to live in the comparative safety of Westcliff in 1942, but who died of cancer at the age of twenty-two months in 1944. My parents, through all this, did their best to ensure that my sister and I continued all our activities …

DANCING DAYS

In 1942 I joined a dancing school and enjoyed learning ballet and tap dancing. We began to do shows in front of small audiences … Our teacher then, called Georgie Johnson, taught us in the front room of her terrace house in Westcliff – not a large space, but she was a good teacher and we were all enthusiastic pupils. Georgie decided we would do something for the war effort and so we were formed into a troop known as The Victory Kids. We entertained other children but our biggest and most important role was in entertaining troops …

Many Wednesday and Saturday evenings were spent doing shows in local church halls to very enthusiastic audiences. You cannot imagine now that soldiers would appreciate being entertained by children as young as three up to about fifteen, but no doubt many of these men were family men who were far from home and missing their own children … if we were doing a tap dance as the guns roared we would tap all the harder to drown out the noise.

Some of our costumes were quite showy, made by mothers … out of former evening dresses etc. We performed one routine called 'George Black's Young Ladies' which was very colourful and my great-aunts produced ostrich feathers which they had worn in their youth to wear as head dresses and also beautiful ostrich feather fans.

We did one particular act where the performers, all little girls, were dressed in eastern costumes and wearing yashmaks over their faces … We were performing at Bournemouth Park Congregational Church one evening and my little sister, then four years old, was dressed as the Sheik complete with cushions to pad her out and wearing a turban and a black beard. On this occasion we had relatives from London in the audience. Imagine their dismay as my sister walked up and down the lines of the harem only to disappear off the back of the stage. She literally bounced with all her cushions, but she let out such a yell …

The entertainment of troops ceased at the end of spring 1944. Many people who lived in the roads of Westcliff and Chalkwell near the seafront were aware of considerable military activity … D-Day had arrived.

CHAPTER THIRTEEN

JOYCE KIPLING

Although Joyce's parents didn't move (from London) to Southend until 1944, Joyce is one of many modest Southenders who played a prominent role in the country's forces. The family moved to Woodcote Road into a house that had been used by the Army, who had worn the treads on the stairs with their hobnail boots.

At this point, Joyce had already been in the WRAF for several years. She started as a cook, baking Yorkshire puddings in buckets (!), and was billeted for a while in what is now Earl's Hall School, also working in the airmen's mess, housed in a former knitting factory near to today's Tesco.

Joyce's high IQ (129) meant that she was moved on to training as a flight mechanic, passing out ACW (Aircraft Woman) 1 with a mark of eighty when the pass was fifty. Her first station was at North Weald, but her wartime experiences covered seventeen different RAF stations over three years – enough for another book!

In fact, every story told here is worthy of a full length book – not just for family historians and local historians, but for national and global historians too.

Joyce Kipling in uniform. (Joyce Kipling collection)

Southend War Memorial. (Author)

SELECT BIBLIOGRAPHY

Age Concern publication, *The Last All Clear* (Sarsen Publishing, Ingatestone, 1989)

Aylen, Steve, *193rd Battery* (self-published, 1999)

Brake, George Thompson, *Leigh Wesley* (The Rochford Press, 1997)

Clamp, Frances, *Southend Voices* (Tempus Publishing Ltd, Stroud, 2004)

Crowe, Ken, *Kursaal Memories* (Skelter Publishing LLP, St Albans, 2003)

Crowe, Ken, *Zeppelins over Southend* (Southend-on-Sea Museums Service publications, 2008)

Easdown, Martin, *Southend Pier* (Tempus Publishing Ltd, Stroud, 2007)

Edwards, Carol, *The Life and Times of the Houseboats of Leigh-on-Sea* (self-published, 2009)

Federation of Essex Women's Institutes publication, *Essex – Within Living Memory* (1995)

Foley, Michael, *Essex: Ready for Anything* (Sutton Publishing, Stroud, 2006)

Foynes, J.P. *The Battle of the East Coast 1939-1945* (self-published, 1994)

Giller, Norman, and Ullyett, Roy, *While There's Still Lead in My Pencil* (Andre Deutsch London, 1998)

Glennie, Donald, *Gunners' Town* (Civic Publications, Southend-on-Sea, 1948)

Gordon, Dee, *People who Mattered in Southend and Beyond* (Ian Henry Publications Ltd, Romford, 2006)

Herbert, A.P. *The War Story of Southend Pier* (Borough of Southend-on-Sea, 1945)

Hill, Tony, *Guns and Gunners at Shoeburyness* (Baron Books, Buckingham, 1999)

Iles, Lesley and Baker, John, *They Rest from their Labours* (published by Southend High School for Boys, 2008)

Jefferies, Malcolm and Lee, J. Alfred, *Hospitals of Southend* (Phillimore & Co. Ltd, Chichester, 1986)

Kelly's Directory, 1916

King, Tom and Furbank, Kevin, *The Southend Story* (published by Southend Standard, 1992)

Roberts, Mark & Rosemary, *Under The Flight Path* (self-published, 1995)

Shepherd, E.W. *The Story of Southend Pier* (Egon Publications, Herts., 1979)

Smith, Graham, *Essex Airfields in the Second World War* (Countryside Books, Newbury, 1996)

Wesley Methodist Church Publication, *A Momentous Century* (1997)

Williams, Judith, *Leigh-on-Sea, A History* (Phillimore & Co Ltd, Chichester, 2002)

Worsdale, Jim, *Southend at War* (self-published, 1997)

Other titles published by The History Press

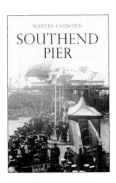

Southend Pier
MARTIN EASDOWN

Southend's pier was constructed in 1830 and, by 1846, was the longest in Europe at over 7,000ft. Millions visited each year but, during 1976, a huge fire engulfed the extensive pierhead. With a fire at the shoreward end in 1977, the pier's existence was in danger but local campaigns to save it have ensured its survival to the present day. Despite another fire and ramming by a ship, life has been breathed back into the pier. This is the story from first construction, through many redevelopments and its current use.

978 0 7524 4215 0

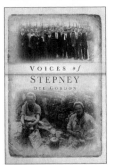

Voices of Stepney
DEE GORDON

This book is the result of many conversations with people who lived and worked in Stepney during the 1950s and '60s. Vivid memories are recounted – focusing particularly on social change. There are memories of Stepney Green, the Royal London Hospital, Charrington's Brewery, Tubby Isaacs, Cable Street, and Brick Lane. Anyone who knows Stepney, as a resident or as a visitor, will be amused and entertained by these stories, which capture the unique spirit of life in the East End.

978 0 7524 5263 0

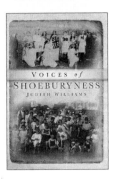

Voices of Shoeburyness
JUDITH WILLIAMS

This book comprises the memories of more than fifty people who lived and worked in Shoeburyness between 1919 and 1970. Many of these memories are shared: long days on the beach, childhood games at 'Bunkers', the tuppenny rush at the Bug Hutch and the folk who lived at Starve Gut. They remember the brickfields, the bargemen, wartime coastal defences, sports at Shoebury Garrison, and 'checkies' on their bicycles.

978 0 7524 5223 4

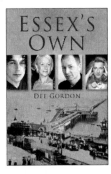

Essex's Own
DEE GORDON

Athlete and TV presenter Sally Gunnell, politician Jack Straw, actress Joan Sims, singer Billy Bragg, footballer Bobby Moore, chef Jamie Oliver, author John Fowles, film director Basil Dearden, playwright Sarah Kane, and the infamous highwayman Dick Turpin are among personalities through the ages who have been born in Essex. The county can claim many more who spent much of their lives here and left their mark on the county, including authors Douglas Adams and Margery Allingham, magician David Nixon and comedian Lee Evans.

978 0 7509 5121 0

Visit our website and discover thousands of other History Press books.

www.thehistorypress.co.uk